Knitted Lace

A COLLECTION OF
FAVORITE DESIGNS
FROM INTERWEAVE

ANNE MERROW

INTERWEAVE
interweave.com

EDITOR Erica Smith

ART DIRECTOR Liz Quan

COVER & INTERIOR DESIGN Julia Boyles

PRODUCTION DESIGN Katherine Jackson

© 2011 Interweave Press LLC
Cover and back cover photography © 2011 Joe Hancock
All rights reserved.

Interweave Press LLC
201 East Fourth Street
Loveland, CO 80537-5655 USA
interweave.com

Printed in China by Asia Pacific Offset, Ltd.

Library of Congress Cataloging-in-Publication Data

Merrow, Anne, 1977–
    Knitted lace : a collection of favorite designs from
Interweave / Anne Merrow.
        p. cm.
    Includes bibliographical references and index.
    ISBN 978-1-59668-482-9 (pbk.)
1. Knitted lace--Patterns. I. Title.
    TT805.K54M47 2011
    746.2'26--dc22

2011002106

10   9   8   7   6   5   4   3   2   1

ACKNOWLEDGMENTS

I am grateful to the staff (past and present) of
Interweave Knits and *Knitscene* magazines, with
particular thanks to Eunny Jang, Lisa Shroyer, Pam
Allen, Laura Rintala, Amy Palmer, Kathy Mallo,
Nancy Arndt, and Dean Howes, for creating the
wonderful magazines from which these patterns and
articles are drawn.

Thanks to the rarely sung heroes of knitting
patterns, the technical editors, whose work is no less
valuable for its near-invisibility.

Jeane Hutchins has collected and preserved so much
lace knitting in the pages of *PieceWork;* thanks for
sharing your knowledge. Thanks also to Karen Brock
for her good humor and hard work throughout the
magazine editorial departments.

Thanks to the Interweave books department for
their tireless efforts, particularly to Julia Boyles for
the lovely design and Mary E. KinCannon for her
organizational skills and good cheer.

My deepest gratitude goes to the indomitable trio of
Ann Budd, Rebecca Campbell, and Kerry Jackson.

CONTENTS

The Infinite Possibilities
OF LACE

There is something uniquely satisfying about knitting lace.

I've seen lots of metaphors for it—a butterfly emerging from a cocoon; a flower blooming—but to my mind, there is enough romance in the simple reality of lace knitting: execute a few easy, repetitive maneuvers with two sticks, and a length of string transforms into delicate, airy fabric traced with pleasingly intricate patterning. For me, the greatest pleasure of knitted lace is in that sense of transformation, of possibility—there's a kind of magic to the idea that such simple building blocks can yield such wonderfully rich effects. The most elaborate lace leaves, waves, and flower petals all come from decreases and yarnovers. Richly ornate geometric motifs are the same, just positive and negative space combined in clever ways. Art underlined with solid knitting logic. Amazing!

And that's just the beginning. The great lace knitting traditions of their world all have their own deep, quirky pools of historical interest and technique innovation. Many lace motifs themselves have fascinating, crooked stories behind them. Then there's the question of what can be made entirely of or adorned with knitted lace—wraps, of course; garments; and any accessory that can be imagined. The actual business of knitting lace entails its own technical know-how. Knitters make choices about the character of lace—because lace is such a heavily manipulated fabric, full of yarnover increases and accompanying decreases, the same lace motif will look dramatically different in different gauges and in different fibers. Lace is a world that unfolds with more and deeper rabbit holes the closer you look.

As the editor of *Interweave Knits*, I've been lucky enough to work and share ideas with knitting designers who are exploring that complex, faceted world—from those steeped in tradition and history to those investigating what lace can do when pushed to its limits. Just as every knitter has her own particular set of factors that go into the projects she chooses, every lace designer has different aims and goals for her designs. Some have clear philosophies expressed in

Wakame Lace Tunic, page 116

Simply Lovely Lace Socks, page 16

Teardrop Scarves, page 32

every project: to bring together traditional techniques and modern wardrobes, say. Some want to explore how they can change an established trend with their signature aesthetic. The mathematicians look for new ways to structure lace or otherwise manipulate expectations. The historians want to celebrate lace from a particular place and time. Ultimately, all want to design something that people want to knit—luckily, there's a lace knitter for every permutation of motif, project, and material.

In this collection, we've looked for designs that span that full range of possibilities, from modern interpretations of deeply traditional ideas such as Evelyn A. Clark's romantic Paisley Lace Shawl and Nancy Bush's Facing Lilies Stole to lighter fare such as Celeste Culpepper's Teardrop Scarves and Karen Baumer's Simply Lovely Lace Socks. We've got snappy, easy garments such as Véronik Avery's sweet Victoria Tank—a simple lace stitch, dressed up with fine detailing—and Kat Coyle's Indigo Ripples Skirt, trimmed in an unfrilly lace stitch and knitted in a denim-dyed

cotton. Some garments are more intricate, patterned all over with a delicate stitch (Shirley Paden's Oriel Lace Blouse) or a combination of lovely lace panels, carefully arranged (Angela Hahn's Wakame Lace Tunic). There are patterns that explore lace's starkly graphic possibilities, such as Mandy Moore's Dorflinger Tee and Donna Druchunas's Arctic Diamonds Stole. There are intricate wraps for romantics, flirty stockings and socks, freshly unfussy tees and hats. The projects span lace traditions from around the world; yarns from cobwebweight alpacas to chunky wools; final effects that range from Victorian elegance to modern punch.

Knitted lace means something different with every project. I hope that as you page through this collection, you feel a sense of discovery and exploration—and the urge to knit.

EUNNY JANG
EDITOR, *Interweave Knits*

A Primer on Knitted Lace

JACKIE ERICKSON-SCHWEITZER

all photos by Jackie Erickson-Schweitzer, Interweave Knits, *Summer 2006*

Airy, light, and a bit mysterious—the delicate tracery of knitted lace is hard to resist. Even the simplest of lace patterns looks impressive and inspires admiration. But intricate as it may appear, knitted lace is simply a fabric punctuated with deliberate openings that can be arranged in a myriad of ways to create patterns that range from basic to complex. The wonderful thing about knitted lace is that in spite of its apparent intricacy, it follows a simple logic. The openings are created by special increases called yarnovers, and each yarnover is accompanied by a compensating decrease. Once you understand how yarnovers and decreases work together, you'll be on your way to mastering the vast array of lace patterns.

Traditional laceweight yarn yields beautiful lace patterns, but sport, worsted, and bulky yarns can be equally effective. A smooth, light-colored fingering or sportweight yarn worked on a needle three to four sizes larger than you'd normally use creates a fluid fabric in which the lace pattern is clearly visible. But fuzzy yarns and dark and variegated colors yield impressive results, too. Experiment with different yarns and needle sizes when you're swatching lace patterns to see the variety of effects you can create with a single pattern; you'll quickly find out what appeals to you.

GETTING STARTED—YARNOVERS AND DECREASES IN A SIMPLE LACE PATTERN

A yarnover is a stitch made by a loop or strand of yarn placed on the right-hand needle as you work. On the return row, this loop is worked as you would any other stitch; once knitted, it leaves a small opening in the knitting.

Each yarnover is counted as an increase of one stitch. To maintain a consistent stitch count, every yarnover is paired with a decrease that may immediately precede or follow the yarnover, appear several stitches away from the yarnover in the same row, or even be worked on a later row. The decreases used in lace knitting are standard: k2tog, ssk, and any of the several kinds of double decreases. The specific kind of decrease to use in any lace pattern is spelled out in its instructions. A good way to see how yarnovers and decreases work together is to knit a sample pattern.

Yarnovers Between Knit Stitches

In the Simple Lace pattern at right, the yarnover is made between two knit stitches and is worked as follows: after knitting the stitch before the yarnover, bring the yarn forward between the needle tips. When you knit the next stitch, bring the yarn up and over the right-hand needle to the back of the work again, ready to knit the next stitch (Figure 1). The strand that travels over the top of the needle is the yarnover, and it counts as one stitch.

Figure 1. Yarnover worked between two knit stitches.

Note that in this pattern, you are working the yarnovers and decreases for lace patterning on the right-side rows. The wrong-side return rows are considered "rest rows" because they are worked without any yarnovers or decreases. Although some lace patterns have patterning on every row, it is quite common for lace patterns to have rest rows that alternate with pattern rows.

Check your work often. If you do discover a mistake, correct it right away. (See page 11 for how to fix mistakes.) After you have knitted a few repeats of the pattern, finish with Row 6 of the repeat and bind off loosely. Pin out the swatch, stretching it so that the pattern formed by the holes is clearly visible. Then steam the swatch.

READING A CHART FOR A SIMPLE LACE PATTERN

Instructions for knitted lace are often presented in chart form. Charts offer a graphic representation of the front or right side of the pattern. The chart at right shows a visual picture of the lace-pattern repeat given in the written instructions above.

Simple Lace Pattern

With size 8 needles and fingering yarn (or any yarn and a pair of larger-than-usual needles), loosely cast on 27 stitches (or any multiple of 9 stitches, the stitch repeat). You may find it helpful to place markers between each 9-stitch repeat.

ROW 1: (RS) *K2, k2tog, yo, k1, yo, ssk, k2; rep from * to end of row.

ROWS 2, 4, 6: (WS) Purl.

ROW 3: *K1, k2tog, yo, k3, yo, ssk, k1; rep from * to end of row.

ROW 5: *K2tog, yo, k1, yo, sl 2 as if to k2tog, k1, pass sl sts over, yo, k1, yo, ssk; rep from * to end of row.

Repeat Rows 1–6 for pattern.

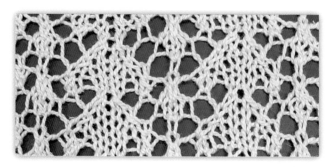

Simple Lace Pattern

☐	k on RS; p on WS
Ⓞ	yo
╱	k2tog
╲	ssk
Λ	sl 2 as if to k2tog, k1, p2sso

Simple Lace Pattern

Each line of the chart represents a row of the stitch pattern. Each square represents a stitch. The chart is read from bottom to top, and RS rows are read from right to left, in the same direction as one normally knits. The first stitch on the left-hand needle as you're ready to begin a row corresponds to the first square in the bottom right-hand corner of the chart. Notice how wrong-side rows have no patterning; they are rest rows. The symbol key tells what to do for each stitch; for example, a plain square represents a knitted stitch and a circle represents a yarnover. A right-slanting line represents k2tog and means that you knit the stitch that corresponds to the k2tog square with the stitch to the left of it.

Note that in this lace pattern, the chart shows that the number of stitches stays the same in each row—for every yarnover, there is a corresponding decrease, and vice versa. On Row 1, the right-slanting k2tog decrease is paired with the yarnover that follows it, and the left-slanting ssk decrease is paired with the yarnover that precedes it. On Row 5, the center double decrease (sl 2 as if to k2tog, k1, pass sl sts over) decreases two stitches, and the yarnovers made on each side of the decrease add two stitches to compensate.

YARNOVERS AND DECREASES IN A BIAS LACE PATTERN

In the Simple Lace pattern, the yarnovers and decreases are balanced. In each repeat, one yarnover falls to the right of its decrease and the other falls to the left of its decrease. Other lace patterns, like the Bias Lace Pattern at right, create zigzag patterns by arranging the yarnovers to fall consistently on one side of their corresponding decreases for several rows before reversing the order.

After you have worked several repeats of the pattern, you'll notice that the edges of the sample are wavy and the stitches

Bias Lace Pattern

Loosely cast on 28 sts (or any multiple of 7 stitches).

ROWS 1, 3, 5, AND 7: (RS) *P1, ssk, k2, yo, k1, p1; rep from * to end.

ALL EVEN-NUMBERED ROWS (2–16): (WS) *K1, p5, k1; rep from * to end.

ROWS 9, 11, 13, AND 15: *P1, k1, yo, k2, k2tog, p1; rep from * to end.

Repeat Rows 1–16 for pattern.

Bias Lace Pattern

tilt away from the vertical to create a bias-lace fabric. The stitches tilt to the right for the first 8 rows because the yarnovers' position to the left of their decreases forces the grain of the fabric to lean to the right. At the same time the fabric angles to the left. On the following 8 rows, the stitches slant to the left because the yarnovers line up to the right of their decreases, and the edges lean to the right. The cast-on edge is slightly scalloped because the yarnover increases and their compensating decreases are separated by other plain stitches.

For your sample, repeat Rows 1–16 twice, then bind off loosely. Notice that the bound-off edge is also slightly wavy due to this separation of yarnovers and compensating decreases, but the scallop is less pronounced than on the cast-on edge. You can increase the scalloped effect of the bind-off row by binding off in pattern and working the decreases extra tight and the yarnovers and stitches on either side of them extra loose.

READING A CHART FOR A BIAS PATTERN AND "NO-STITCH" SYMBOLS

As mentioned above, one advantage of a lace chart is that it shows a rough picture of the actual knitted fabric. Charts for bias patterns with wavy edges employ a "no-stitch" symbol, which is simply a placeholder that's usually represented by a gray square. You don't do anything when you see a gray no-stitch symbol. You only knit according to the symbols represented by the white squares.

Compare the chart at left to the written instructions for the bias lace pattern. The instructions and the chart tell you how to knit the same lace pattern, but the chart gives a visual picture of how the lace will look.

Besides bias patterns, there are other types of lace that may use the no-stitch symbol in charts. Examples include patterns with stitch counts that vary from row to row (a yarnover's compensating decrease is deferred until a later row in the pattern), some lace edgings, and certain garment shapes.

YARNOVERS WORKED BETWEEN DIFFERENT TYPES OF STITCHES

Whether knits or purls precede or follow a yarnover determine the way it's made. In the Simple Lace pattern, the yarnovers always fall between two knit stitches. The three other yarnovers are made as follows:

Yarnover Between a Knit and a Purl

(Working yarn begins in back.) Bring the yarn to the front of work between needles. Then bring the strand of yarn over the needle and through the needles again to the front—wrapping the needle—and ready to purl the next stitch (Figure 2).

Bias Lace Pattern

	k on RS; p on WS
•	p on RS; k on WS
Ⓞ	yo
╱	k2tog
╲	ssk
	no stitch

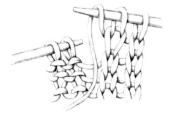

Figure 2. Yarnover worked after a knit and before a purl stitch.

Mixed Knit-Purl Lace

To practice the different yarnovers, work this variation of the Simple Lace pattern. Cast on 27 sts (or any multiple of 9 stitches).

ROW 1: (RS) *P2, k2tog, yo, p1, yo, ssk, p2; rep from * to end.

ROW 2: *K2, p2, k1, p2, k2; rep from * to end.

ROW 3: *P1, k2tog, yo, p3, yo, ssk, p1; rep from * to end.

ROW 4: *K1, p2, k3, p2, k1; rep from * to end.

ROW 5: *K2tog, yo, p1, yo, p3tog, yo, p1, yo, ssk; rep from * to end.

ROW 6: *P2, k5, p2; rep from * to end.

Repeat Rows 1–6 for pattern.

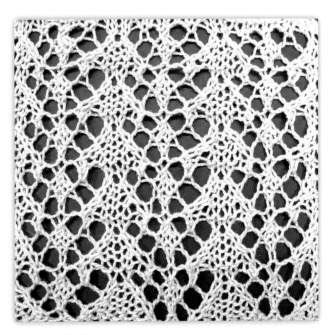

Mixed Knit-Purl Lace

Yarnover Between a Purl and a Knit

(Working yarn begins in front.) Bring the strand of yarn over the right-hand needle to the back and knit the next stitch (Figure 3).

Figure 3. Yarnover worked after a purl and before a knit stitch.

Yarnover Between a Purl and a Purl

(Working yarn begins in front.) Bring the strand of yarn over the right-hand needle to the back and to the front again between the tips of the needles—wrapping the needle— ready to purl the next stitch (Figure 4).

Figure 4. Yarnover worked between two purl stitches.

Work the Mixed Knit-Purl Lace pattern to see the variety of yarnover possibilities. Complete Row 6 of the last pattern repeat and bind off loosely. Block the sample. Compare this variation to the Simple Lace Pattern to see how changing knit stitches to purls varies the pattern.

COMMON MISTAKES AND GETTING BACK ON TRACK

If you discover a mistake, take a breath and stay calm. Even expert knitters make mistakes. The most common mistakes in lace knitting are fairly easy to fix.

> If you forgot to make a yarnover, identify where you omitted the yarnover and temporarily mark that spot with a removable marker or safety pin. On the return row, insert the right-hand needle from back to front under the running thread (the strand directly between and below the two needles), pick it up and place it on the left-hand needle ready to take the place of the missing yarnover.

> If you make an extra yarnover, on the return row drop the extra loop and continue on. At first that area will look a bit looser, but blocking will even out any irregularities.

> If the pattern design doesn't look right or the stitch count is off, and you can't identify the problem, unwork stitches one by one across the row. Recheck your stitch count until you get to a place where the pattern works properly again, then proceed.

Using a Lifeline

A lifeline is a temporary thread inserted through a row of stitches that serves as a checkpoint if you need to rip out and redo several rows. Here's how to make a lifeline:

1. Decide on a lifeline row. A good choice is an unpatterned rest row at the beginning or end of a pattern repeat, for example Row 6 in our first lace-pattern example.

2. After completing the designated row, thread a fine, smooth thread (crochet thread works well) in a contrasting color onto a tapestry needle and run it through the bottom of each stitch on the needle, but not through any markers. Pull the lifeline thread out on each side of the row, leaving tails at least 6" (15 cm) hanging down on each side. When you resume knitting, be careful not to knit the lifeline into the new stitches you make.

With luck, you'll never need to use the lifeline. But if you discover a mistake, remove the knitting needle and ravel down to the lifeline thread. With a smaller size knitting needle, pick up stitches along the lifeline thread by inserting the needle tip through each stitch held by the lifeline; follow the lifeline thread to pick up all the stitches in the original marked row so that they are mounted on the needle properly. Do not remove the lifeline. Count the stitches to be sure that you have the number you should have on the designated lifeline row. Then resume knitting with the original size needles.

Preventing Mistakes

Practicing a few good habits will make it easy to work even the trickiest lace pattern.

> Be sure that you can easily read and keep your place in the instructions. Enlarge charts and, if necessary, transcribe texts or charts into terminology or symbols that work for you.

> Use a magnetic strip, ruler, or Post-it just above the row you are working. Doing so helps your eyes focus on that row while it allows you to check previously knitted rows as a reference point.

> Create good working conditions: increase lighting, minimize distractions, and avoid knitting when you are tired.

> Check your work often: count stitches, use markers liberally, and visually compare your knitting against any available charts and sample photographs.

> Read the pattern out loud as you work through the pattern the first few times. Simultaneous seeing, hearing, and doing can be helpful.

Seine
SCARF

FINISHED SIZE

7½" (19 cm) wide and 56" (142 cm) long, after blocking.

YARN

Laceweight (Lace #0).

SHOWN HERE: Twisted Sisters Impressionist Zazu (100% merino; 390 yd [356 m]/50 g): ballerina blues, 1 skein. Yarn distributed by Yarnmarket.com.

NEEDLES

U.S. size 5 (3.75 mm). Adjust needle size if necessary to obtain the correct gauge.

NOTIONS

Markers (m); tapestry needle.

GAUGE

13 sts and 15 rows = 2" (5 cm) in lace patt st, after blocking; 12 sts and 19 rows = 2" (5 cm) in St st, before blocking.

Ann Budd
Interweave Knits Weekend, 2009

The strong diagonal lines of this scarf make it the perfect choice to show off a solid or variegated yarn—such as a skein of special sock yarn. The easy-to-memorize stitch pattern makes this a good first lace pattern or a delightful respite for experienced lace knitters.

Scarf

CO 47 sts.

Bottom Edging

Work Edging chart Rows 1 and 2 three times, then rep Edging Row 1 once more—7 rows total.

INC ROW: (WS) K1, p2, M1 (see Glossary), purl to last st, k1—48 sts.

Body

Rep Rows 1–16 of Diagonal Lace chart until piece measures 54½" (133.5 cm) from CO, or about 1½" (3.8 cm) less than desired total length, ending with Row 13 of chart.

DEC ROW: (WS) K1, p1, p2tog, purl to last st, k1—47 sts rem.

Top Edging

Rep Rows 1 and 2 of Edging 4 times—8 rows total.

BO all sts as foll: K2tog, *replace st on left needle, k2tog through back loops; rep from * until 1 st rem. Cut yarn and pull tail through rem loop.

Finishing

Block to measurements, pinning out points in bottom and top edging. Weave in loose ends.

☐	k on RS; p on WS
☐•	p on RS; k on WS
☐╱	k2tog
☐╲	ssk
☐Ｏ	yo
☐⋀	sl 2 tog kwise, k1, p2sso
▨	no stitch
●	stitch marker
☐	pattern repeat
▨	border sts

Edging

Diagonal Lace

8 st repeat

SEINE SCARF

FINISHED SIZE

7½" (19 cm) foot circumference, 4" (10 cm) long from cast-on edge to top of heel flap, and 9" (23 cm) long from back of heel to tip of toe. To fit women's U.S. shoe sizes 8 to 9.

YARN

Sportweight or fingering weight (Fine #2 or Super Fine #1).

SHOWN HERE: Louet Gems Sport Weight (100% merino; 225 yd [206 m]/100 g): willow, 1 skein, or Louet Gems Fingering Weight (100% merino; 172 yd [157 m]/50 g): pink panther, 2 skeins. (See Notes on page 18 regarding yarn selection.)

NEEDLES

U.S. size 3 (3.25 mm) or size 0 (2 mm): set of 5 double-pointed (dpn) plus 1 extra. (See Notes on page 18 to determine needle size.) Adjust needle size if necessary to obtain the correct gauge.

NOTIONS

Marker (m); tapestry needle.

GAUGE

25 sts and 34 rnds = 4" (10 cm) worked in St st in the rnd on size 3 (3.25 mm) needles with sportweight. 32 sts and 43 rnds = 4" (10 cm) worked in St st in the rnd on size 0 (2 mm) needles with fingering weight.

Simply Lovely
LACE SOCKS

Karen Baumer
Interweave Knits, SPRING 2006

This pretty but very simple lace pattern offers a change of pace from traditional ribbed socks, without requiring elaborate charts or unwavering attention. Choose a fingering-weight yarn and work a picot edge for a dainty version, or choose a sportweight yarn and a basic ribbed cuff for a quick-to-knit pair.

NOTES

This pattern is written for two weights of yarn; the green sock is knitted in a sportweight yarn, and the pink sock, the alternative yarn, in a fingering-weight yarn. Instructions for sportweight appear first and instructions for fingering weight appear in parentheses. When no parentheses are present, the directions apply to both weights of yarn. Work fingering weight on size 3 (3.25 mm) needles and fingering weight on size 0 (2 mm) needles (or size needed to obtain respective gauge).

The foot of the sock is worked with one fewer stitch than the cuff in order to maintain a balanced pattern on the instep. The stitch count is readjusted during the first round of toe decreases.

The ribbed cuff of the sportweight sock may also be used for the fingering-weight version, but the picot edge cuff should not be used on the sportweight version, as the heavier yarn would create excessive bulk when folded double.

Legend

□	k
b	k tbl
O	yo
λ	sl 1, k2tog, psso
□ (bold)	pattern repeat

Instep

b				b	b	b				b
b				b	b	b				b	(3)
b	O	λ	O	b	b	b	O	λ	O	b
b				b	b	b				b	(1)

Leg

			b	b	b
			b	b	b	(3)
O	λ	O	b	b	b
			b	b	b	(1)

Sock

Cuff

Loosely CO 48 (60) sts onto 1 dpn. Divide sts evenly onto 4 dpns (12 [15] sts each needle), place marker (pm), and join for working in the rnd, being careful not to twist sts.

Work the cuff of your choice as foll:

SPORTWEIGHT CUFF
Work [k1, p1] rib for for ¾" (2 cm).

FINGERING WEIGHT PICOT CUFF
Redistribute sts as foll: 14 sts on Needles 1 and 3; 16 sts on Needles 2 and 4.

Knit 5 rnds.

PICOT RND: *K2tog, yo; rep from * to end of rnd.

Knit 5 rnds.

Redistribute stitches as foll: 15 sts per needle.

BOTH VERSIONS
Work Leg chart until cuff measures 4" (10 cm) from CO edge or picot rnd, ending with Rnd 4 of chart.

Heel

HEEL FLAP
With Needle 4, knit the first st on Needle 1 through the back loop (tbl). With an empty needle, *sl 1, k1; rep from * 12 (15) times—24 (30) heel sts on one needle.

Work heel sts back and forth in rows as foll:

ROW 1: (WS) Sl 1, purl to end.

ROW 2: *Sl 1, k1; rep from * to end.

Rep Rows 1 and 2 twelve (eighteen) times—heel flap measures about 2½" (6.5 cm) from beg; 12 (18) slipped selvedge sts along each side of heel flap.

TURN HEEL
Work short-rows as foll:

ROW 1: (WS) Sl 1, p12 (15), p2tog, p1, turn.

ROW 2: (RS) Sl 1, k3, ssk, k1, turn.

ROW 3: Sl 1, purl to 1 st before gap on prev row, p2tog, p1, turn.

ROW 4: Sl 1, knit to 1 st before gap on prev row, ssk, k1, turn.

Rep Rows 3 and 4 until all heel sts have been worked, ending with a RS row—14 (16) sts rem.

SHAPE GUSSETS
Work in rnds as foll:

RND 1: With Needle 1, pick up and knit (see Glossary) 12 (18) sts along left edge of heel flap; with Needle 2, k2tog tbl (counts as first st of Instep chart), work Instep chart across Needle 2 and Needle 3; with Needle 4, pick up and knit 12 (18) sts along right side of heel flap, then knit 7 (8) heel sts from Needle 1 again—61 (81) sts total; 19 (26) sts each on Needle 1 and Needle 4; 23 (29) instep sts distributed between Needle 2 and Needle 3. Rnd begins at center of heel.

RND 2: Needle 1—k7 (8), [k1 tbl] 12 (18) times; Needles 2 and 3—cont instep patt as established; Needle 4—[k1 tbl] 12 (18) times, k7 (8).

RND 3: Needle 1—knit to last 3 sts, k2tog, k1; Needles 2 and 3—cont instep patt; Needle 4—k1, ssk, knit to end—59 (79) sts rem.

RND 4: Knit, maintaining instep patt on Needles 2 and 3.

Rep Rnds 3 and 4 until 47 (59) sts rem (see Notes)—12 (15) sts each on Needles 1 and 4; 23 (29) instep sts distributed between Needles 2 and 3.

Foot

Work even in patt, working sole in St st and instep in patt as established, until foot measures 7¼" (18.5 cm) or 1¾" (4.5 cm) less than desired total length, ending after Needle 4 (center of heel).

Toe

Adjust sts so that there are 11 (14) sts on Needle 2 and 12 (15) sts each on Needles 1, 3, and 4. Knit 1 rnd.

DEC RND: Needle 1—knit to last 3 sts, k2tog, k1; Needle 2—knit; Needle 3—knit to last 3 sts, k2tog, k1; Needle 4—k1, ssk, knit to end—44 (56) sts rem.

Knit 1 rnd even. Cont in rnds as foll:

RND 1: Needle 1—knit to last 3 sts, k2tog, k1; Needle 2—k1, ssk, knit to end; Needle 3—knit to last 3 sts, k2tog, k1; Needle 4—k1, ssk, knit to end.

RND 2: Knit.

Rep Rnds 1 and 2 until 24 (28) sts rem, then rep Rnd 1 only until 12 sts rem.

Finishing

With Needle 4, k3 from Needle 1. Sl sts from Needle 3 onto Needle 2—6 sts each on 2 needles. Cut yarn, leaving a 12" (30.5 cm) tail. With tail threaded on a tapestry needle, use Kitchener st (see Glossary) to graft sts tog. Weave in loose ends. Block lightly.

Picot Cuff Only

Fold cuff to WS at picot rnd and, with yarn threaded on a tapestry needle, loosely tack CO to inside of sock.

SIMPLY LOVELY LACE SOCKS

Oneshot
LACE HAT

Hana Jason
Interweave Knits, SUMMER 2009

Unexpected, simple, charming—lace can work in all kinds of ways. Hana Jason was inspired by the idea of lace moving around a curve to create this elegant three-season accessory. Spiraling short-row wedges in a simple garter lace create a pinwheel effect that shows off a slightly glitzy yarn in an unconventional, subtle way.

FINISHED SIZE

18" (45.5 cm) circumference at brim, to fit a woman's medium. Hat is very stretchy.

YARN

Worsted weight (Medium #4).

SHOWN HERE: Gedifra Amara (80% cotton, 20% polyamide; 110 yd [100 m]/50 g): #3719 khaki, 1 ball.

NEEDLES

U.S. sizes 8 (5 mm) and 4 (3.75 mm): 16" (40 cm) circulars (cir). Adjust needle size if necessary to obtain the correct gauge.

NOTIONS

Tapestry needle.

GAUGE

20 sts = 4" (10 cm) and 14 rows = 2" (5 cm) in pattern st; each wedge measures 7" (18 cm) long and 2" (5 cm) wide at widest point (brim).

NOTES

You can make a larger, deeper hat by working an additional short-row wedge. Each wedge added or removed changes the brim circumference by 2" (5 cm).

Hat

With larger cir needle and the invisible provisional method (see Glossary), CO 36 sts.

Short-row Wedge

Note: See diagram at right.

ROW 1: (RS) Sl 1, *yo, k2tog; rep from * to last st, turn, leaving last st unworked.

ROWS 2, 4, 6, 8, 10, AND 12: (WS) Knit to end.

ROW 3: Sl 1, k1, *yo, k2tog; rep from * to last 4 sts, turn.

ROW 5: Sl 1, *yo, k2tog; rep from * to last 7 sts, turn.

ROW 7: Sl 1, k1, *yo, k2tog; rep from * to last 10 sts, turn.

ROW 9: Sl 1, *yo, k2tog; rep from * to last 13 sts, turn.

ROW 11: Sl 1, k1, *yo, k2tog; rep from * to last 16 sts, turn.

ROW 13: Knit across all sts.

ROW 14: (WS) Sl 1, knit to end.

Rep Rows 1–14 eight more times—9 wedges total.

Finishing

Cut yarn, leaving a 30" (76 cm) tail. Remove provisional CO and place revealed sts on needle. With tapestry needle, use Kitchener st (see Glossary) to graft sts tog.

Band

With smaller needle, pick up and knit 1 st in each slipped st along brim edge for a total of 112 sts. Join in the rnd. Work in k1tbl, p1 rib for 3 rnds. BO all sts in rib. Sew hole at crown of hat closed. Weave in ends. Block, opening up lace. Stretch firmly for a slouchy cap or only gently for a tight hat as shown.

Wedge 1

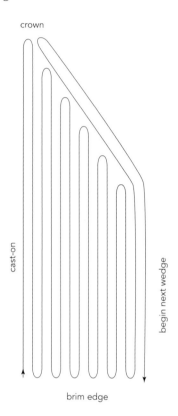

crown

cast-on

begin next wedge

brim edge

ONESHOT LACE HAT

Arctic Diamonds
STOLE

FINISHED SIZE
21" (53.5 cm) wide and 48" (122 cm) long, after blocking.

YARN
Fingering weight (Super Fine #1).

SHOWN HERE: Louet Gems Fingering Weight (100% merino; 172 yd [157 m]/50 g): terra cotta, 6 skeins.

NEEDLES
U.S. size 3 (3.25 mm). Adjust needle size if necessary to obtain the correct gauge.

NOTIONS
Blocking board; rust-proof pins or blocking wires; tapestry needle.

GAUGE
24 sts and 32 rows = 4" (10 cm) in charted patt, after blocking.

Donna Druchunas
Interweave Knits, WINTER 2006

A geometric arrangement of framed diamonds ripples along the body of this sweeping lace stole. Donna Druchunas drew inspiration for her lace pattern from a pieced motif she saw on the trim of a furry Alaskan parka. The stole is a variation on a project from her book *Arctic Lace: Knitting Projects and Stories Inspired by Alaska's Native Knitters.*

Stole

CO 130 sts. Work Rows 1–13 of Beginning Edging chart—131 sts. Work Rows 1–10 of Parka-Trim Diamond chart once, Rows 11–74 five times, and Rows 75–101 once (ending with a RS row). Work Rows 1–13 of Ending Edging chart. BO all sts loosely.

Finishing

Weave in loose ends.

Blocking

Wet stole thoroughly. Using the lines on a blocking board to ensure straight edges, stretch the stole to the finished measurements and secure with pins or blocking wires. Allow stole to dry thoroughly before unpinning.

Parka-Trim Diamond (Rows 75–101)

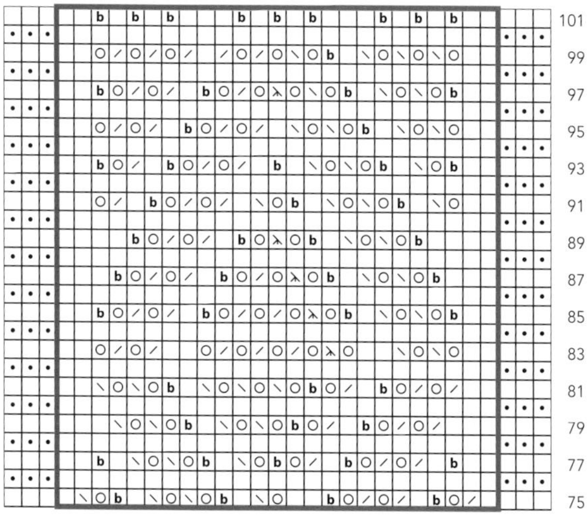

101
99
97
95
93
91
89
87
85
83
81
79
77
75

Parka-Trim Diamond (Rows 1–74)

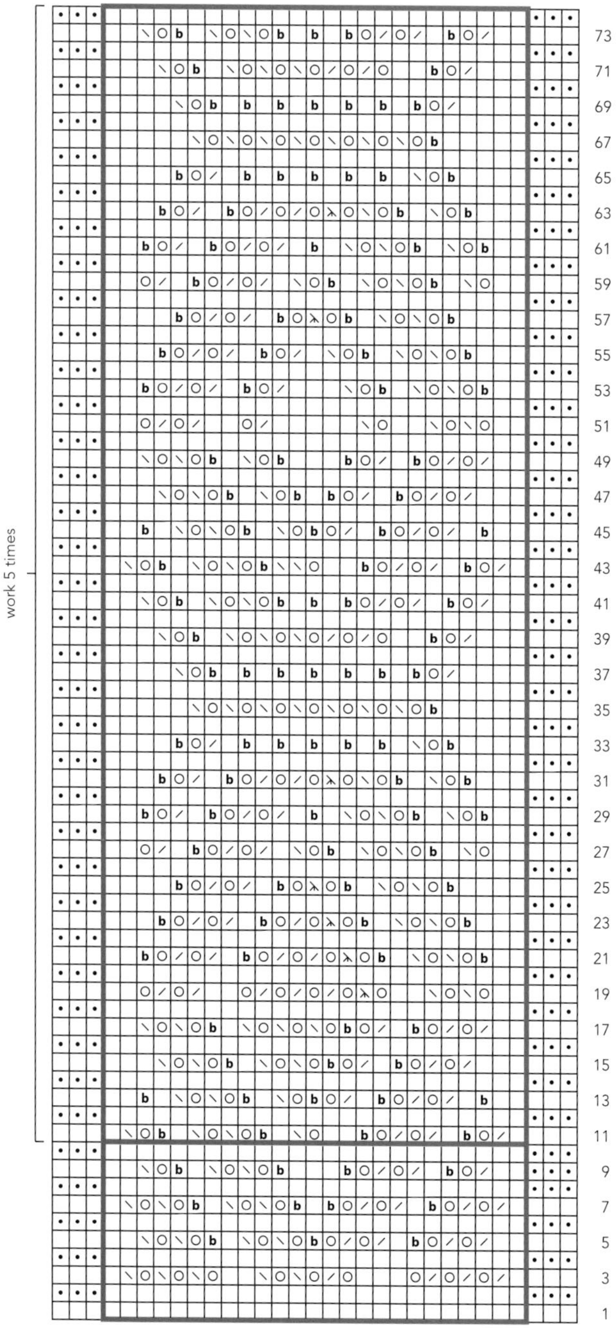

work 5 times

73
71
69
67
65
63
61
59
57
55
53
51
49
47
45
43
41
39
37
35
33
31
29
27
25
23
21
19
17
15
13
11
9
7
5
3
1

Beginning Edging

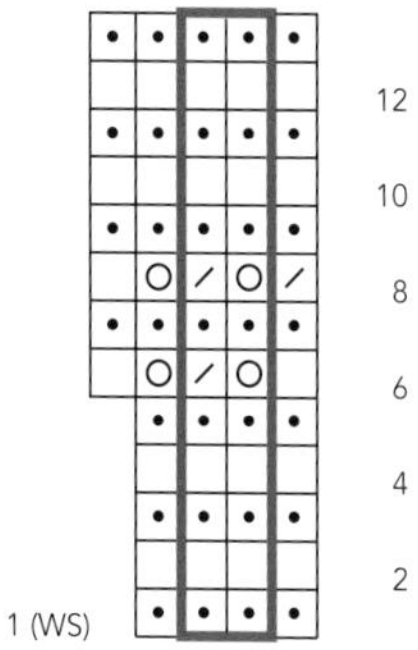

12
10
8
6
4
2

1 (WS)

Ending Edging

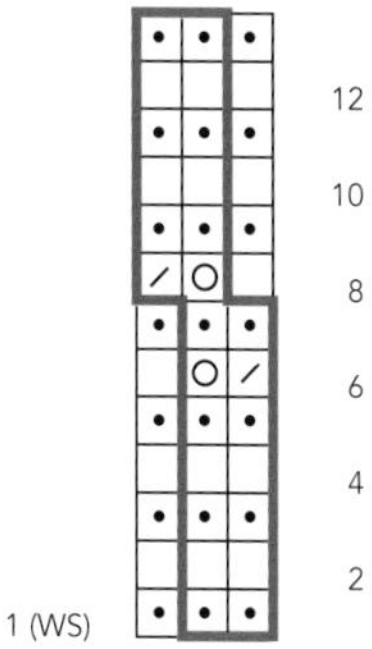

12
10
8
6
4
2

1 (WS)

☐ k on RS; p on WS	╲ k2tog tbl
• p on RS; k on WS	⋌ sl 1 kwise, k2tog, psso
☐ yo	b k tbl
╱ k2tog	☐ pattern repeat

Swallowtail
SHAWL

Evelyn A. Clark
Interweave Knits, FALL 2006

A simple bud lace pattern makes up the body of this little shawl. The pattern flows into a deep lily-of-the-valley border with a peaked edging. From the few stitches that form the center of the base of the triangle, the shawl is shaped by columns of yarnovers along the center spine and edges. The shawl is worked in a light as a feather laceweight alpaca that shows every detail of the intricate patterning.

FINISHED SIZE
23" (58.5 cm) from bottom center point to top edge and 49" (124.5 cm) wide across top edge, after blocking.

YARN
Laceweight (Lace #0).

SHOWN HERE: Misti Alpaca Lace (100% baby alpaca; 437 yd [400 ml]/50 g): #7120 sea mist, 1 ball.

NEEDLES
U.S. size 4 (3.5 mm). Adjust needle size if necessary to obtain the correct gauge.

NOTIONS
Marker (m); safety pin; rustproof pins for blocking; size E/4 (3.5 mm) crochet hook; waste yarn in contrasting color.

GAUGE
17½ sts and 17½ rows = 4" (10 cm) in Budding Lace patt after blocking.

NOTES

The first and last 2 stitches of every row are worked in garter st for top edge border.

....

The shawl increases 4 stitches every other row until Row 11 of edging.

....

It is helpful to place a stitch marker after the yarnover and before the center stitch and to place a safety pin along side edge to mark beginning of odd-numbered rows.

....

The shawl can be made larger by working it with fingering, sport, or worsted-weight yarn on larger needles.

Shawl
Top Border

Beg at center back neck, work crochet chain provisional CO (see Glossary) as foll: Using crochet hook and waste yarn, ch 4, fasten off. With shawl yarn and knitting needles, pick up and knit (see Glossary) 1 st in each of 2 bumps at back of chain—2 sts.

ROWS 1–6: Knit.

ROW 7: K2, pick up and knit 1 st in each of 3 garter ridges along side edge; unzip waste yarn chain, putting the 2 exposed sts onto left needle; knit these 2 sts—7 sts.

Work Rows 1–10 of Budding Lace 1 chart—27 sts.

Work Rows 1–6 of Budding Lace 2 chart 14 times—195 sts.

Work Rows 1–12 of Lily of the Valley Border 1 chart—219 sts.

Work Rows 1–10 of Lily of the Valley Border 2 chart—239 sts.

Work Rows 1–16 of Peaked Edging chart—259 sts.

NEXT ROW: (RS) K2, *yo, k7, yo, k1; rep from * to last st, k1—323 sts.

NEXT ROW: (WS) Knit.

BO as foll: K2, *return both sts to left needle and k2tog through back loop (tbl), k1; rep from * until all sts have been bound-off.

Finishing

Weave in loose ends, but do not trim tails until after blocking.

Blocking

Soak shawl for at least 20 minutes. Wrap in towel to remove excess water. Lay flat and smooth into shape. If using blocking wires, run through eyelets along top edge and pin. Pull out points along side edges at each yo, k1, yo and pin. Leave in place until thoroughly dry. Trim yarn ends.

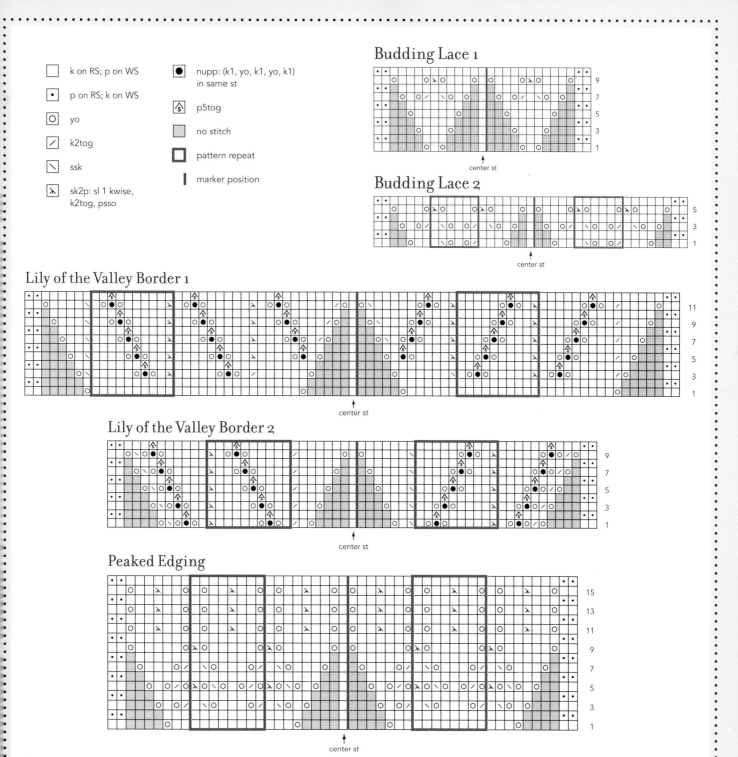

Budding Lace 1

Budding Lace 2

Lily of the Valley Border 1

Lily of the Valley Border 2

Peaked Edging

Legend:
- ☐ k on RS; p on WS
- ・ p on RS; k on WS
- ☐O yo
- / k2tog
- \ ssk
- ⋏ sk2p: sl 1 kwise, k2tog, psso
- ● nupp: (k1, yo, k1, yo, k1) in same st
- ⑤ p5tog
- ☐ no stitch
- ☐ pattern repeat
- | marker position

center st

Teardrop
SCARVES

Celeste Culpepper
Knitscene, FALL 2007

FINISHED SIZE

Blue scarf: 8" (20.5 cm) wide and
51" (129.5 cm) long, after blocking;
Pink scarf: 8" (20.5 cm) wide and 72"
(183 cm) long, after blocking.

YARN

Laceweight (Lace #0).

SHOWN HERE: Jade Sapphire Lacey
Lamb (100% lambswool; 825 yd
[755 m]/60 g): #309 slate blue or #202
soft pink, 1 skein.

NEEDLES

U.S. size 3 (3.25 mm): 32" (80 cm)
circular (cir) needle. Adjust needle
size if necessary to obtain the correct
gauge.

NOTIONS

93 beads per scarf—Blue scarf:
4 × 6mm teardrops in Pearl Fuchsia;
Pink scarf: 3.44mm White Pearl AB
drops; dental floss threader; tapestry
needle.

GAUGE

19 sts and 47 rows = 4" (10 cm) in patt,
after blocking.

These lace scarves, shown in two lengths, are worked
sideways in long rows. Shaping at each short end creates
a scalloped edge, which is tipped with glass beads. The
method for placing the beads uses an unexpected tool—a
dental floss threader—to avoid stringing all the beads
at the beginning of the project. The yarn's flowing
elegance belies the easy patterning.

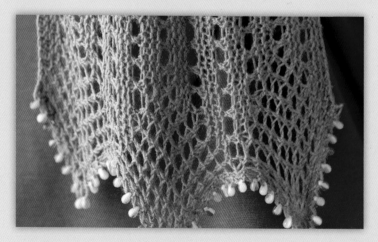

STITCH GUIDE

Place Bead (PB) Using a Dental Floss Threader

Dental floss threaders can be purchased at most drugstores. The bright blue threaders, which look like tiny tennis racquets without the inside strings, come in a package of ten to twenty threaders. Take a dental floss threader and pull on each side of its loop. The threader will separate into one long strand.

Cut both ends of the threader so you have a 6" (15 cm) length, shaped like the letter U. Thread it through the stitch as if to knit, bring both ends of the threader together, and remove this threaded stitch from your left-hand needle. Using the two ends of the threader held together, thread these ends through the hole in the bead. Push the bead down the threader and over the stitch. The loop of the stitch is now between the bead and the threader. Place this beaded stitch on the right-hand needle without working it, making sure that its orientation is correct.

NOTES

Stitch count changes throughout, creating the scalloped look on the scarf ends.

....

Work a yarnover at the beginning of a row by bringing the yarn over the top of the right needle before working k2tog.

....

Sources: beads shown from www.earthfaire.com

Scarf

Blue scarf: CO 226 sts. **Pink scarf:** CO 326 sts. Do not join.

ROW 1: Knit.

ROW 2: Yo, k2tog, k1, yo, knit to end.

ROW 3: Yo, k2tog, k1, yo, knit to last st, PB (see Stitch Guide on page 34).

ROWS 4 AND 5: Yo, k2tog, k1, yo, k2tog, yo, knit to last st, PB.

ROWS 6 AND 7: Yo, k2tog, k1, [yo, k2tog] 2 times, yo, knit to last st, PB.

ROW 8: Yo, k2tog, k1, [yo, k2tog] 3 times, yo, k2, *yo, k2tog; rep from * to last 9 sts, k8, PB.

ROW 9: Yo, k2tog, k1, [yo, k2tog] 3 times, yo, knit to last st, PB.

ROWS 10 AND 11: Yo, k2tog, k1, [yo, k2tog] 4 times, yo, knit to last st, PB.

ROWS 12 AND 13: Yo, k2tog, k1, [yo, k2tog] 5 times, yo, knit to last st, PB.

ROWS 14 AND 15: Yo, k2tog, k1, [yo, k2tog] 6 times, yo, knit to last st, PB.

ROW 16: Yo, k2tog, k1, [yo, k2tog] 7 times, yo, *k2tog, yo; rep from * to last 17 sts, k16, PB.

ROW 17: Yo, k2tog, k1, [yo, k2tog] 7 times, yo, knit to last st, PB.

ROWS 18 AND 19: Yo, [k2tog] 2 times, [yo, k2tog] 7 times, knit to last st, PB.

ROWS 20 AND 21: Yo, [k2tog] 2 times, [yo, k2tog] 6 times, knit to last st, PB.

ROWS 22 AND 23: Yo, [k2tog] 2 times, [yo, k2tog] 5 times, knit to last st, PB.

ROW 24: Yo, [k2tog] 2 times, [yo, k2tog] 4 times, k1, *yo, k2tog; rep from * to last 13 sts, k12, PB.

ROW 25: Yo, [k2tog] 2 times, [yo, k2tog] 4 times, knit to last st, PB.

ROWS 26 AND 27: Yo, [k2tog] 2 times, [yo, k2tog] 3 times, knit to last st, PB.

ROWS 28 AND 29: Yo, [k2tog] 2 times, [yo, k2tog] 2 times, knit to last st, PB.

ROWS 30 AND 31: Yo, [k2tog] 2 times, yo, k2tog, knit to last st, PB.

ROW 32: Yo, [k2tog] 2 times, k1, *yo, k2tog; rep from * to last 5 sts, k4, PB.

ROW 33: Yo, [k2tog] 2 times, knit to last st, PB.

ROW 34: Yo, k2tog, k1, yo, knit to last st, PB.

Work Rows 3–34 once more, then rep Rows 3–30 once more.

NEXT ROW: [K2tog] 3 times, knit to last st, PB.

NEXT ROW: (BO row) [K2tog] 2 times, pass first st over second to BO very loosely to last 2 sts, k2tog, BO rem st.

Finishing

Weave in ends. Soak scarf in warm water and a gentle wool wash. Wrap in towel and squeeze out excess water. Lay flat and pin to finished size.

Isis
WRAP

FINISHED SIZE
35½ (40, 47½)" (90 [101.5, 120.5] cm) bust circumference, tied. Sweater shown measures 40" (101 cm).

YARN
Worsted weight (Medium #4).

SHOWN HERE: Tahki New Tweed (70% merino, 15% silk, 11% cotton, 4% viscose; 103 yd [95 m]/50 g): #018 blue, 5 (6, 8) balls.

NEEDLES
Size 9 (5.5 mm). Adjust needle size if necessary to obtain the correct gauge.

NOTIONS
Removable markers (m) or safety pins; stitch holders; tapestry needle.

GAUGE
17 sts and 24 rows = 4" (10 cm) in lace patt.

Kathleen Power Johnson
Interweave Knits, SUMMER 2005

A kimono sleeve creates a smooth shoulder line in this brief summer sweater with a lace pattern reminiscent of rippling water. The fronts and back are worked separately from the lower edges to the armhole, then stitches are cast on and worked for the sleeves. Ribbed front ties allow for an adjustable fit; work longer ties for a wraparound version of the sweater.

STITCH GUIDE

Selvedge Stitches

Unless otherwise specified, slip the first st of every row (kwise for knit sts, pwise for purl sts); knit the last st of every row.

....

Lace Pattern: (multiple of 8 sts + 3)

ROW 1: (RS) K1, *k2, yo, ssk, k1, k2tog, yo, k1; rep from * to last 2 sts, k2.

ROWS 2, 4, AND 6: (WS) Purl.

ROW 3: K1, *k1, yo, ssk, yo, sl 2 tog kwise, k1, p2sso, yo, k2tog, yo; rep from * to last 2 sts, k2.

ROWS 5 AND 7: K1, *k1, yo, sl 2 tog kwise, k1, p2sso, yo; rep from * to last 2 sts, k2.

ROW 8: Purl.

Repeat Rows 1–8 for pattern.

NOTES

If there are not enough stitches as a result of shaping to work a yarnover or decrease with its companion decrease or yarnover, work the stitches in stockinette stitch until there are enough stitches to resume working in pattern.

Wrap

Back

CO 69 (77, 93) sts. Work in k1, p1 rib until piece measures 1" (2.5 cm), ending with a WS row. Establish selvedge sts and lace patt on next row as foll: (RS) Sl 1 (selvedge st; see Notes at left), work Row 1 of lace patt over center 67 (75, 91) sts, k1 (selvedge st). Work 1 WS row even.

SHAPE SIDES
NEXT ROW: (RS) Sl 1, M1 (see Glossary), work in patt to last st, M1, k1.

Work 3 rows even.

Rep last 4 rows 1 (2, 2) more time(s), then work inc row once more—75 (85, 101) sts; 11 (15, 15) patt rows completed, ending with Row 3 (7, 7) of patt.

Work 1 WS row even—piece measures about 3 (3¾, 3¾)" (7.5 [9.5, 9.5] cm) from beg.

SHAPE SLEEVES
Using the knitted method (see page 55), CO 2 sts at beg of next 8 (10, 14) rows, then CO 3 sts at beg of foll 2 (4, 6) rows, then CO 5 sts at beg of foll 4 rows, then CO 6 sts at beg of

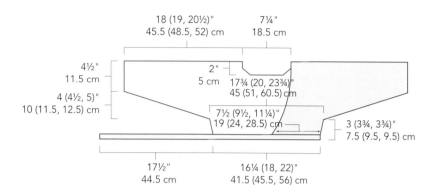

foll 2 (2, 4) rows, then CO 7 sts at beg of foll 8 (6, 2) rows, working CO sts into patt—185 (191, 205) sts; piece measures about 7 (8¼, 8¾)" (18 [21, 22] cm) from beg. Mark each end of last row completed with safety pin or scrap yarn to indicate end of sleeve shaping. Work even in patt for 2½" (6.5 cm) beyond sleeve markers, ending with a WS row—piece should measure about 9½ (10¾, 11¼)" (24 [27.5, 28.5] cm) from beg.

SHAPE BACK NECK

Cont in patt, work 82 (85, 92) sts, join new yarn and BO 21 sts for neck, work to end of row—82 (85, 92) sts at each side. Working each side separately, at each neck edge BO 5 sts once—77 (80, 87) sts rem each side. Cont even in patt until piece measures 11½ (12¾, 13¼)" (29 [32.5, 33.5] cm) from beg, or about 4½" (11.5 cm) from sleeve markers for all sizes, ending with a RS row. BO all sts.

Right Front

CO 106 (114, 122) sts. Work k1, p1 rib until piece measures 1" (2.5 cm), ending with a WS row.

NEXT ROW: (RS) BO 74 sts for tie (1 st rem on right needle), work next 3 sts in established rib, pm, work Row 1 of lace patt over next 27 (35, 43) sts, k1 (selvedge st)—32 (40, 48) sts.

NEXT ROW: (WS) Sl 1 (selvedge st), work in patt to last 4 sts, work 4 sts in rib. *Note:* The side, neck, and sleeve shaping are worked at the same time; read the next section all the way through before proceeding.

Keep 1 st at side edge (end of RS rows; beg of WS rows) as a selvedge st and maintain 4 sts at center front edge (beg of RS rows; end of WS rows) in k1, p1 rib; do not slip the first st of the ribbed edging on RS rows.

SHAPE SIDE, FRONT NECK, AND SLEEVES

Beg with the next RS row (Row 3 of patt), inc 1 st at side edge inside selvedge st every 4th row 3 (4, 4) times total, and *at the same time* dec 1 st at neck edge inside rib sts every 4th row 3 (4, 4) times, ending with Row 3 (7, 7) of patt—still 32 (40, 48) sts; 11 (15, 15) patt rows completed; side shaping is finished for all sizes.

Cont to dec 1 st at neck edge inside rib sts every 4th row 6 (9, 9) more times, and *at the same time,* beg with the next WS row, shape sleeve as foll: use the cable method (see page 55) to CO 2 sts at beg of next 4 (5, 7) WS rows, then CO 3 sts at beg of foll 1 (2, 3) WS row(s), then CO 5 sts at beg of foll 2 WS rows, then CO 6 sts at beg of foll 1 (1, 2) WS row(s), then

CO 7 sts at beg of foll 4 (3, 1) WS row(s), working CO sts in patt. Mark cuff edge of last sleeve CO row to indicate end of sleeve shaping, about 7 (8¼, 8¾)" (18 [21, 22] cm) from beg. When all neck and sleeve shaping has been completed, there will be 81 (84, 91) sts—55 (53, 52) sts CO for sleeve; 6 (9, 9) more sts dec'd at neck edge.

Work even until piece measures 11½ (12¾, 13¼)" (29 [32.5, 33.5] cm) from beg, or about 4½" (11.5 cm) from sleeve marker, ending with a RS row.

NEXT ROW: (WS) BO 77 (80, 87) sts, place rem 4 sts of rib band on holder.

Left Front

CO 106 (114, 122) sts. Work in k1, p1 rib until piece measures 1" (2.5 cm), ending with a RS row.

NEXT ROW: (WS) BO 74 sts for tie, work in rib patt to end—32 (40, 48) sts.

NEXT ROW: (RS) Sl 1 (selvedge st), pm, work Row 1 of lace patt over next 27 (35, 43) sts, pm, work 4 sts in rib. Work 1 WS row even. *Note:* The side, neck, and sleeve shaping are worked at the same time; please read the next section all the way through before proceeding.

Keep 1 st at side edge (beg of RS rows, end of WS rows) as a selvedge st and maintain 4 sts at center front edge (end of RS rows, beg of WS rows) in k1, p1 rib; do not slip the first st of the ribbed edging on WS rows.

SHAPE SIDE, FRONT NECK, AND SLEEVES
Beg with the next RS row (Row 3 of patt), inc 1 st at side edge inside selvedge st every 4th row 3 (4, 4) times total, and *at the same time* dec 1 st at neck edge inside rib sts every 4th row 3 (4, 4) times, ending with Row 3 (7, 7) of patt—still 32 (40, 48) sts; 11 (15, 15) patt rows completed; side shaping is finished for all sizes. Work 1 WS row even.

Cont to dec 1 st at neck edge inside rib sts every 4th row 6 (9, 9) more times, and *at the same time*, beg with the next RS row, use the knitted method to shape sleeve as foll: CO 2 sts at beg of next 4 (5, 7) RS rows, then CO 3 sts at beg of foll 1 (2, 3) RS row(s), then CO 5 sts at beg foll 2 RS rows, then CO 6 sts at beg of foll 1 (1, 2) RS row(s), then CO 7 sts at beg of foll 4 (3, 1) RS row(s), working CO sts in patt. Mark cuff edge of last sleeve CO row to indicate end of sleeve shaping, about 7 (8¼, 8¾)" (18 [21, 22] cm) from beg—81 (84, 91) sts when all neck and sleeve shaping has been completed.

Work even until piece measures 11½ (12¾, 13¼)" (29 [32.5, 33.5] cm) from beg, or about 4½" (11.5 cm) from sleeve marker, ending with a WS row.

NEXT ROW: (RS) BO 77 (80, 87) sts, place rem 4 sts of rib band on holder.

Finishing

With yarn threaded on a tapestry needle, sew shoulder and side seams.

Right Neckband

Return 4 held sts from right front to needle and join yarn with RS facing.

ROW 1: (RS) Work 4 sts in rib, pick up and knit 1 st from neck edge—5 sts.

ROWS 2 AND 4: Work even in rib, working picked-up st in patt.

ROW 3: Work established rib to end, pick up and knit 1 st from neck edge—6 sts.

ROW 5: Work 4 sts in rib, ssk, pick up and knit 1 st from neck edge—still 6 sts.

ROW 6: Work in established rib.

Cont to rep Rows 5 and 6 until band reaches center back when slightly stretched. Cut yarn, leaving a 14" (35.5 cm) tail. Place sts on holder.

Left Neckband

Return 4 held sts from left front to needle and join yarn with WS facing.

ROW 1: (WS) Work 4 sts in rib, pick up and purl 1 st from neck edge—5 sts.

ROWS 2 AND 4: Work even in rib, working picked-up st in patt.

ROW 3: Work established rib to end, pick up and purl 1 st from neck edge—6 sts.

ROW 5: Work 4 sts in rib, p2tog, pick up and purl 1 st from neck edge—still 6 sts.

ROW 6: Work in established rib.

Rep Rows 5 and 6 until band reaches center back when slightly stretched. Cut yarn and place sts on holder. With tail threaded on a tapestry needle, use the Kitchener st (see Glossary) to join bands tog at center back, adding or removing rows to adjust length of bands if necessary. Weave in loose ends. Block lightly.

ISIS WRAP

Slanting Plaid
STOLE

Rachel Erin
Interweave Knits, FALL 2010

Clever knitting gives a lightweight fabric deep dimension in this striking, graphic stole. A sideways braid stitch, borrowed from ganseys and mittens, creates a square grid reminiscent of windowpane plaid, while simple lace textures—which subtly alternate directions within the squares—suggest twill weave structures.

FINISHED SIZE
22" (56 cm) wide and 78" (198 cm) long, excluding fringe.

YARN
Laceweight (Lace #0).

SHOWN HERE: The Alpaca Yarn Company Suri Elegance (100% alpaca; 875 yd [800 m]/100 g): #2008 cordovan, 3 skeins.

NEEDLES
U.S. size 5 (3.75 mm). Adjust needle size if necessary to obtain the correct gauge.

NOTIONS
Blocking wires or cotton crochet thread; 7" (18 cm) piece of cardboard for making fringe; tapestry needle.

GAUGE
18 sts and 26 rows = 4" (10 cm) in lace patt with yarn doubled, after blocking.

STITCH GUIDE

Bias Square Lace: (multiple of 36 sts + 26)

ROW 1: (RS) Sl 2, *ssk, yo 2 times, k2tog, [yo, ssk] 7 times, ssk, yo 2 times, k2tog, [k2tog, yo] 7 times; rep from * once more, ssk, yo 2 times, k2tog, [yo, ssk] 7 times, ssk, yo 2 times, k2tog, k2.

ROWS 2 AND 4: Sl 2, purl to end, working (k1, p1) into each double yo.

ROW 3: Sl 2, *ssk, yo 2 times, k2tog, k1, yo, [ssk, yo] 6 times, sl 2 as if to k2tog, k1, p2sso, yo 2 times, sl 2 as if to k2tog, k1, p2sso, [yo, k2tog] 6 times, yo, k1; rep from * once more, ssk, yo 2 times, k2tog, k1, yo, [ssk, yo] 6 times, sl 2 as if to k2tog, k1, p2sso, yo 2 times, k2tog, k2.

Rep Rows 1–4 for patt.

....

Sideways Stitch Stripe: (multiple of 3 sts + 2)

Note: Be careful to treat each loop of the double yo as one stitch.

ROWS 1 AND 3: (WS) Sl 2, p1f&b, *sl first st on right needle to left needle, purl 2nd st on left needle but don't drop st off, then purl first st on left needle, dropping both sts off; rep from * to last 3 sts, sl first st on right needle to left needle, p2tog, p2.

ROW 2: Sl 2, ssk, *yo 2 times, sl 2 as if to k2tog, k1, p2sso; rep from * to last 4 sts, yo 2 times, k2tog, k2.

NOTES

Work with two strands of yarn held together throughout.

....

While working, the squares will be tilted. They are blocked square during finishing.

Knitted Lace

Stole

With yarn doubled and working over two needles, CO 98 sts. Remove one needle from CO.

*Work Rows 1–3 of Sideways St Stripe (see Stitch Guide at left).

Work Rows 1–4 of Bias Square Lace (see Stitch Guide) 6 times, then work Row 1 once more.

Rep from * 17 more times, or until piece measures ½" (1.3 cm) less than desired finished length. Work Rows 1 and 2 of Sideways St Stripe.

Loosely BO all sts as foll: Sl 2, pass 2nd st on right needle over first to BO 1 st, p1f&b, *sl first st on right needle to left needle, pass 2nd st on right needle over first to BO 1 st, purl 2nd st on left needle but don't drop st off, then purl first st on left needle, dropping both sts off; rep from * to last 3 sts, sl first st on right needle to left needle, pass 2nd st on right needle over first, p2tog, pass 2nd st on right needle over first, [p1, pass 2nd st on right needle over first] 2 times. Fasten off last st.

Finishing

Block to measurements. Use cotton thread or blocking wires to help block each small square on the inside of the stole to 4" (10 cm). Weave in loose ends.

Fringe

Using the piece of cardboard, wrap the yarn repeatedly around it. Cut one end of the loops, making many 14" (35.5 cm) long strands. Rep as necessary as you run out of strands. You will need 784 strands total. For each CO and BO st, hold 4 strands tog and thread onto a tapestry needle, then pull strands through st. Fold strands in half, matching ends, and tie in an overhand knot. Trim even, if necessary, to 6" (15 cm).

SLANTING PLAID STOLE

Fountain Pen
SHAWL

FINISHED SIZE
78" (198 cm) wide at top edge and 39" (99 cm) long, measured down center line, after blocking.

YARN
Laceweight (Lace #0).

SHOWN HERE: Lorna's Laces Helen's Lace (50% silk, 50% wool; 1250 yd [1143 m]/113 g): #9NS pewter, 1 skein.

NEEDLES
Size 6 (4 mm): straight or 24" (60 cm) circular (cir). Adjust needle size if necessary to obtain the correct gauge.

NOTIONS
Coil-less safety pin; tapestry needle; T-pins for blocking.

GAUGE
16 sts and 24 rows = 4" (10 cm) in St st, after blocking.

Susan Pierce Lawrence
Interweave Knits, SPRING 2009

Lace goes literary in this triangular shawl, which features a motif in the shape of a classic fountain pen nib. The pattern gets its dimensions from curving lozenges punctuated with eyelets and nupps. After trying several edging variations, designer Susan Pierce Lawrence settled on a simple pattern that accents but doesn't compete with the strong curving lines of the basic design.

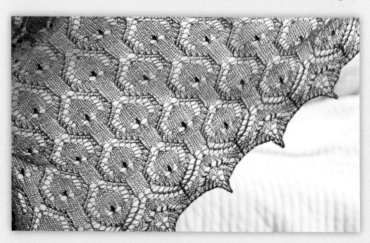

Nupp

(K1, yo, k1, yo, k1) in same st.

NOTES

This shawl is worked from the center back of the neck down to the bottom edge. The main body of the shawl is worked first, followed by the bottom border. The triangular shape is created by working yarnover increases on the inside of the garter stitch borders and on each side of the center stitch. These increases are worked on right-side rows only. Use a coil-less safety pin to mark the center stitch. No other markers are necessary, although you may choose to place one before and after the two-stitch garter borders. If using additional markers, remove them before working Border Chart. To minimize errors, it is helpful to count your stitches as you work each wrong-side row. The stitch count increases by four stitches each time you complete a right-side row, there is always an odd number of stitches on each side of the center stitch, and the total stitch count is always an odd number.

Because the bottom border flows directly from the main stitch pattern, the shawl can easily be made larger or smaller by working more or fewer repeats of the Body chart before beginning the Border chart. The sample shawl used about 77 grams (2.7 ounces) of the recommended yarn. Increasing the size of the shawl will require more yarn.

Shawl

Using the knitted method (see page 55), CO 5 sts.

Set up patt:

ROWS 1 AND 2: Knit.

ROW 3: K2, yo, k1 (center st), yo, k2—7 sts.

Mark center st using coil-less safety pin and move up work as needed.

ROW 4: K2, p3, k2.

Body

Work Rows 1–20 of Lace Beginning chart once—47 sts. Work Rows 1–16 of Body chart 10 times—367 sts.

Lower Border

Work Rows 1–24 of Border chart once—415 sts.

Bind Off

Note: This two-step BO ensures a stretchy bottom edge that blocks easily. Work Row 2 loosely.

ROW 1: (RS) K2, yo, k14, [yo, k1, yo, k15] 11 times, yo, k1, yo, k14, yo, k1 (center st), yo, k14, [yo, k1, yo, k15] 11 times, yo, k1, yo, k14, yo, k2—467 sts.

ROW 2: K1, *k1, insert tip of left needle into the front of the 2 sts on the right needle and knit them tog; rep from * until all sts are BO.

Finishing

Weave in loose ends but do not trim. Soak shawl in cool water until thoroughly wet. Gently squeeze out the excess water, then place the shawl between two towels and press firmly to remove additional water. Block by pinning the damp shawl to a flat surface, pulling the points out along the bottom edge. Do not remove the pins until the shawl is completely dry. Trim yarn ends.

Legend

- □ k on RS; p on WS
- • p on RS; k on WS
- ○ yo
- ╱ k2tog
- ╲ ssk
- ▲ sl 2 as if to k2tog, k1, p2sso
- nupp (see Stitch Guide)
- p5tog
- (gray) no stitch
- □ pattern repeat

Lace Beginning

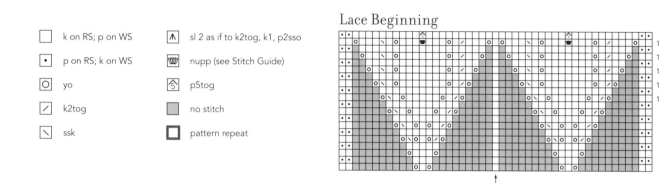

center st

Body

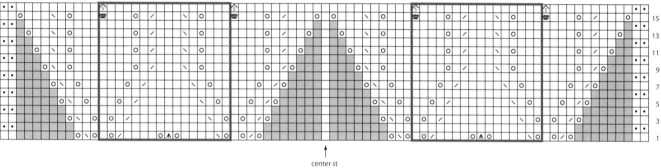

center st

Border

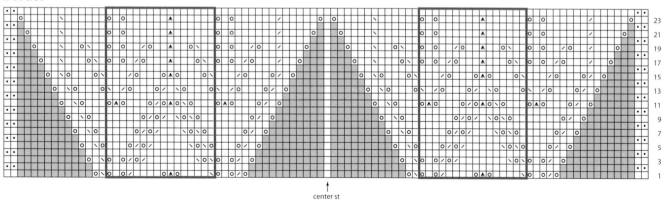

center st

FINISHED SIZE

26¾ (29¾, 32, 35, 37¼)" (68 [75.5, 81.5, 89, 94.5] cm) waist circumference and 37 (40, 42¼, 45¼, 47½)" (94 [101.5, 107.5, 115, 120.5] cm) hip circumference, measured about 9" (23 cm) below waist. Skirt shown measures 37" (94 cm) at hip.

YARN

Worsted weight (Medium #4).

SHOWN HERE: Garnstudio Den-M-Nit (100% cotton; 100 yd [92 m]/50 g): #51 indigo-dyed cotton, 8 (9, 10, 11, 12) skeins. Yarn distributed by Aurora Yarns. *Note: Den-M-Nit is currently available from Elann.com; alternatively, try Rowan Denim.*

NEEDLES

Size 6 (4 mm): 24" (60 cm) and 29" (70 cm) circulars (cir) and 2 double-pointed (dpn).

NOTIONS

Markers (m); tapestry needle; size F/5 (3.75 mm) crochet hook.

GAUGE

21 sts and 27 rnds = 4" (10 cm) in St st in the rnd, before washing; 21 sts and 30 rnds = 4" (10 cm) in St st after washing; about 21 sts and 26 rnds = 4" (10 cm) in lace patt, after blocking or washing.

Indigo Ripples
SKIRT

Kat Coyle
Interweave Knits, SPRING 2007

Indigo Ripples looks at the jeans skirt from a knitterly angle. A denim yarn, unfrilly lace pattern, and a small, flippy ruffle combine in an unusual knitted version of the wardrobe staple. Like classic blue jeans, this skirt can be dressed up or down for timeless style, versatility, and comfort.

NOTES

This skirt is worked from the waist down, in the round. The skirt is designed to be worn at the natural waist; therefore, the shaped section between waist and full hip makes up nearly half the skirt's length.

....

Like blue jeans, this skirt will change in length when washed and dried; keep the finished measurements in mind when choosing a size.

Skirt

CO 140 (156, 168, 184, 196) sts. Place marker (pm) for center back and join for working in the rnd, being careful not to twist sts.

Eyelet Waistband

RNDS 1 AND 2: Knit.

RND 3: *K2, yo, k2tog; rep from * around.

RNDS 4 AND 5: Purl.

Main Body

RND 1: K35 (39, 42, 46, 49), pm, use the backward-loop method (see page 55) to CO 1 st, pm, k70 (78, 84, 92, 98), pm, CO 1 st, pm, k35 (39, 42, 46, 49)—142 (158, 170, 186, 198) sts.

Work 3 rnds even in St st.

NEXT RND: (inc rnd) *Knit to next m, M1R (see Glossary), sl m, knit to next m, sl m, M1L (see Glossary); rep from * once, knit to end of rnd—4 sts inc'd.

Rep inc rnd every 4th rnd 8 more times—178 (194, 206, 222, 234) sts.

Work inc rnd every 6th rnd 3 times, then on the foll 8th rnd 1 time—194 (210, 222, 238, 250) sts.

Work 7 rnds even.

NEXT RND: *Knit to next m, M1R 1 (0, 1, 0, 1) time, sl m, knit to next m, sl m; rep from * once, knit to end of rnd—196 (210, 224, 238, 252) sts.

Work even in St st until piece measures 12½" (31.5 cm) from end of waistband, removing all m except beg-of-rnd m; piece will measure about 11¼" (28.5 cm) from end of waistband after washing.

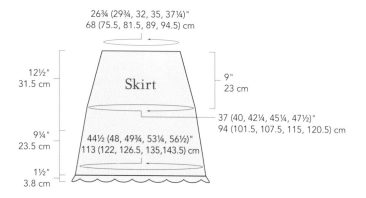

26¾ (29¾, 32, 35, 37¼)"
68 (75.5, 81.5, 89, 94.5) cm

12½"
31.5 cm

Skirt

9"
23 cm

37 (40, 42¼, 45¼, 47½)"
94 (101.5, 107.5, 115, 120.5) cm

9¼"
23.5 cm

44½ (48, 49¾, 53¼, 56½)"
113 (122, 126.5, 135,143.5) cm

1½"
3.8 cm

Lace Section

RNDS 1 AND 3: *Yo, k3, sl 1, k2tog, psso, yo, k1, yo, k3tog, k3, yo, k1; rep from * to end.

RND 2 AND ALL EVEN-NUMBERED RNDS: Knit.

RND 5: (inc rnd) *Yo, k3, sl 1, k2tog, psso, yo, k1, yo, k3tog, k1, M1R, k2, yo, k1; rep from * to end—210 (225, 240, 255, 270) sts.

RNDS 7, 9, 21, AND 23: *Yo, k3, sl 1, k2tog, psso, yo, k1, yo, k3tog, k4, yo, k1; rep from * to end.

RNDS 11, 13, 15, 17, AND 19: *Yo, k3tog, k3, yo, k1, yo, k4, sl 1, k2tog, psso, yo, k1; rep from * to end.

RND 25: (inc rnd) *Yo, k1, M1R, k2, sl 1, k2tog, psso, yo, k1, yo, k3tog, k4, yo, k1; rep from * to end—224 (240, 256, 272, 288) sts.

RNDS 27, 29, 41, 43, 45, 47, AND 49: *Yo, k4, sl 1, k2tog, psso, yo, k1, yo, k3tog, k4, yo, k1; rep from * to end.

RNDS 31, 33, 35, 37, 39, 51, 53, 55, 57, AND 59: *Yo, k3tog, k4, yo, k1, yo, k4, sl 1, k2tog, psso, yo, k1; rep from * to end.

RND 60: K2 (0, 1, 3, 0), *k22 (20, 51, 38, 32), M1R; rep from * to last 2 (0, 0, 3, 0) sts, k2 (0, 0, 3, 0)—234 (252, 261, 279, 297) sts.

Ruffle

RND 1: Purl.

RND 2: *K1, yo; rep from * to end—468 (504, 522, 558, 594) sts.

RNDS 3 AND 4: Knit.

RND 5: *[K2tog] 6 times, [yo, k1] 6 times; rep from * to end.

RND 6: Knit.

RNDS 7–10: Rep Rnds 3–6.

RND 11: Purl.

BO as foll: K1, *use the knitted method (see page 55) to CO 1 st onto left needle, BO 2 sts; rep from * to end.

Drawstring

With dpn, CO 3 sts. Work I-cord (see Glossary) for 51 (54, 57, 60, 63)" (129.5 [137, 145, 152.5, 160] cm). BO all sts.

Finishing

Weave in loose ends. Handwash skirt in lukewarm water; roll skirt in towels, squeezing out excess water. Block skirt to measurements, pinning ruffled hem at long scalloped edges and gently pulling to open holes in lace sections. Length in the lace section can be blocked from 9" (23 cm) to 10½" (26.5 cm). Beg at center front, weave drawstring through eyelets in waistband and tie in bow.

Casting On & Binding Off Lace

EUNNY JANG

Adapted from "A Primer on Knitted Lace: Part Two," Interweave Knits, *Fall 2006*

Knitted lace, a fabric that consists largely of holes, will always stretch wider than its counterpart in stockinette or garter stitch. The most common methods of casting on and binding off, however, often produce an edge that's too firm and inflexible to stretch the width of a lacy fabric.

Traditional lace shawls were often designed to avoid this problem by doing away with cast-on or bound-off edges altogether. A provisional cast-on and a "live" last row allowed the piece to be finished off with a perpendicular knitted edging. But many of today's lace projects—simple lace scarves and shawls, for example—are knitted from a permanent cast-on edge to the bind-off row. The following cast-on and bind-off methods yield flexible edges with enough give to accommodate the most aggressive blocking.

CASTING ON

A Note on the Long-Tail Cast-On

Conventional wisdom for increasing the elasticity of a cast-on edge has the knitter work the long-tail (Continental) method over two needles. Unfortunately, this modification doesn't provide a more elastic edge: the stitches on the needle may be larger, but the size of the knots at the base of the stitches remains the same. Only a very little yarn is used in each "knot" and between neighboring knots, yielding the same tight and inelastic edge.

To compensate, the knitter must somehow add extra yarn either to each knot formed at the base of the stitch or between knots. Leave a consistent length of yarn (¼"–½" [6–13 mm], depending on the gauge of the piece) between each stitch as you cast on, or use June Hiatt's ingenious double-needle cast-on to enlarge the knots themselves. Although her book, *The Principles of Knitting: Methods and Techniques of Hand Knitting,* is out of print, copies may be available at your local library, through interlibrary loan, or through the Internet.

Backward-Loop Cast-On

The backward-loop cast-on works beautifully for lace fabric because of its absolute simplicity—there are no twists or knots on the cast-on row of stitches. But it may stretch even more than the body stitches and must be pinned carefully during blocking to avoid flared or scalloped edges.

Make a loop with the working yarn and place it on the needle backward. The loops may be made with the ball end of the yarn in front or in back of the loop. The difference is almost impossible to see once worked, though you may prefer a forward loop (Figure 1) when the first row after cast-on is knitted and a backward loop (Figure 2) when it's purled.

Figure 1   *Figure 2*

Knitted Cast-On

More solid than a backward-loop cast-on, the knitted cast-on produces an edge that is lacy and loopy and will stretch as far as you need it to. Though instructions for this cast-on often start with a slipknot loop, for a completely knotless edge, try a simple twisted loop instead.

Place a twisted loop (or slipknot) on the left needle. Knit into this stitch with the right needle (Figure 1), draw a new stitch through, and place it on the left needle (Figure 2). Repeat until the correct number of stitches has been cast on, always knitting into the last stitch you made.

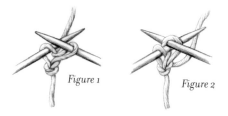

Figure 1   *Figure 2*

Cable Cast-On

If there are no stitches on the needles, make a slipknot of working yarn and place it on the needle, then use the knitted method to cast on one more stitch—two stitches on needle. Hold needle with working yarn in your left hand with the wrong side of the work facing you. *Insert right needle between the first two stitches on left needle (Figure 1), wrap yarn around needle as if to knit, draw yarn through (Figure 2), and place new loop on left needle (Figure 3) to form a new stitch. Repeat from * for the desired number of stitches, always working between the first two stitches on the left needle.

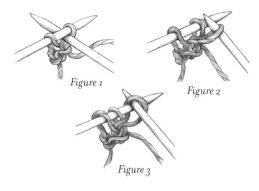

Figure 1   *Figure 2*

Figure 3

Emily Ocker's Circular Beginning

Make a simple loop of yarn with the short end hanging down. With a crochet hook, *draw a loop through main loop, then draw another loop through this loop. Repeat from * for each stitch to be cast on. After several inches have been worked, pull on the short end to tighten the loop and close the circle.

BINDING OFF

Many lace patterns, after pages of intricate charts and working instructions, end abruptly with a note to "bind off loosely." Although the standard k1, psso bind-off may be loosened slightly by working it with a needle many sizes larger than those used for the body, it still may not have the necessary give to stretch comfortably with the fabric. The following variations on binding off may be a little more awkward to work, but the results are worth it.

Standard Bind-Off

Knit the first stitch, *knit the next stitch (two stitches on right needle), insert left needle tip into first stitch on right needle (Figure 1) and lift this stitch up and over the second stitch (Figure 2) and off the needle (Figure 3). Repeat from * for the desired number of stitches.

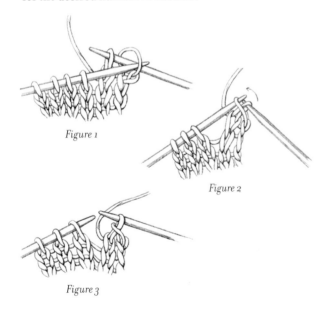

Figure 1

Figure 2

Figure 3

Modified Standard Bind-Off

If working with very large needles doesn't produce a bind-off with enough elasticity, a little extra yarn can be manually inserted as you work. Bind off as usual, making a yarnover between stitches at regular intervals (Figure 1) and slipping it over with the stitch being bound-off (Figure 2). Depending on how open and airy the body stitch is—and how far it needs to stretch—a yarnover may be inserted between every third, second, or even after every stitch.

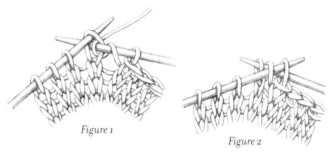

Figure 1

Figure 2

Suspended Bind-Off

Another variation on the standard method, this provides more stretch by inserting extra yarn in the bind-off. Slip one stitch, knit one stitch, *insert left needle tip into first stitch on right needle and lift the first stitch over the second, keeping the lifted stitch at the end of the left needle (Figure 1). Skipping the lifted stitch, knit the next stitch (Figure 2), then slip both stitches off the left needle—two stitches remain on right needle and one stitch has been

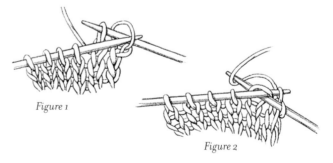

Figure 1

Figure 2

bound off (Figure 3). Repeat from * until no stitches remain on left needle, then pass first stitch on right needle over second.

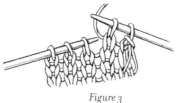

Figure 3

Elizabeth Zimmerman's Sewn Bind-Off

This sewn bind-off, which Elizabeth Zimmerman described in her book *Knitting Without Tears* (Fireside, 1973), mirrors the look of a cast-on row. Worked with carefully matched tension, it makes a tidy bound-off edge.

Break working yarn, leaving at least 1½" (3.8 cm) for every stitch to be bound off. Thread the yarn into a blunt tapestry needle small enough to pass through the live stitches without stretching them. Insert the tapestry needle into the first stitch on the needle as if to knit, and slip this stitch off the knitting needle. *Insert the tapestry needle purlwise into the next two stitches, leaving them on the knitting needle (Figure 1), and pull the yarn through. Insert the tapestry needle into the first stitch on the needle as if to

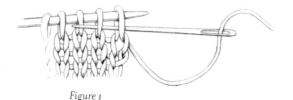

Figure 1

knit (Figure 2), and slip this stitch off the needle. Repeat from * until all stitches have been bound off.

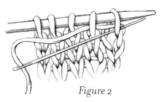

Figure 2

Lace Bind-Off

Sometimes called a Russian bind-off, the yielding—but very strong—edge this method creates is ideal for edges that are to be blocked into points or scallops. Though the bind-off row is worked with purl stitches, it looks right at home on the right side of a stockinette fabric—a good thing, because a bind-off worked in this way with knit stitches doesn't have the same elasticity.

Purl two stitches. *Slip the two stitches back onto the left needle, without twisting (Figure 1). Purl two together (Figure 2), purl one stitch (Figure 3). Repeat from * until one stitch remains; break yarn and pull through to finish.

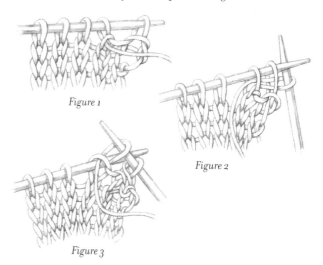

Figure 1

Figure 2

Figure 3

FINISHED SIZE

32½ (34½, 37, 39½, 42, 44½, 47, 49½, 52, 54½)" (82.5 [87.5, 94, 100.5, 106.5, 113, 119.5, 125.5, 132, 138.5] cm) chest/bust circumference. Tank shown measures 34½" (87.5 cm).

YARN

Fingering weight (Super Fine #1).

SHOWN HERE: Schoeller Esslinger Fortissima Cotton (75% cotton, 25% polyamide; 230 yd [210 m]/50 g): #01 white 3 (3, 4, 4, 4, 5, 5, 5, 6, 6) balls. *Note: This yarn has been discontinued; try substituting Schoeller Fortissima Socka Cotton.*

NEEDLES

BODY: U.S. size 3 (3.25 mm): 24" or 32" (60 or 80 cm) circular (cir).

EDGING: U.S. size 2 (2.5 mm): 16" (40 cm) cir. Adjust needle size if necessary to obtain the correct gauge.

NOTIONS

Markers (m); size B/1 (2.5 mm) crochet hook; tapestry needle.

GAUGE

29 sts and 34 rows = 4" (10 cm) in vine lace patt worked in the rnd on larger needles.

Victoria
TANK

Véronik Avery
Interweave Knits, **SUMMER 2004**

This pretty tank, worked in the round in an easily memorized pattern, is the ideal project for knitters who want to try an allover lace garment. The shoulder straps continue the edging patterns around the arms and neck finished off with a delicate picot edge that emerges from two sides of a provisional cast-on.

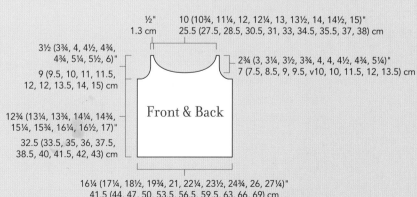

½"
1.3 cm

10 (10¾, 11¼, 12, 12¼, 13, 13½, 14, 14½, 15)"
25.5 (27.5, 28.5, 30.5, 31, 33, 34.5, 35.5, 37, 38) cm

3½ (3¾, 4, 4½, 4¾, 4¾, 5¼, 5½, 6)"
9 (9.5, 10, 11, 11.5, 12, 12, 13.5, 14, 15) cm

2¾ (3, 3¼, 3½, 3¾, 4, 4, 4½, 4¾, 5¼)"
7 (7.5, 8.5, 9, 9.5, v10, 10, 11.5, 12, 13.5) cm

12¾ (13¼, 13¾, 14¼, 14¾, 15¼, 15¾, 16¼, 16½, 17)"
32.5 (33.5, 35, 36, 37.5, 38.5, 40, 41.5, 42, 43) cm

Front & Back

16¼ (17¼, 18½, 19¾, 21, 22¼, 23½, 24¾, 26, 27¼)"
41.5 (44, 47, 50, 53.5, 56.5, 59.5, 63, 66, 69) cm

STITCH GUIDE

Vine Lace in rnds: (multiple of 9 sts)

RNDS 1 AND 3: Knit.

RND 2: *K1, yo, k2, ssk, k2tog, k2, yo; rep from *.

RND 4: *Yo, k2, ssk, k2tog, k2, yo, k1; rep from *.

Repeat Rnds 1–4 for pattern.

· ·

Vine Lace in rows: (multiple of 9 sts)

ROWS 1 AND 3: (WS) Purl.

ROW 2: *K1, yo, k2, ssk, k2tog, k2, yo; rep from *.

ROW 4: *Yo, k2, ssk, k2tog, k2, yo, k1; rep from *.

Repeat Rows 1–4 for pattern.

NOTES

If there are not enough sts as the result of shaping to work a yarnover or decrease with its companion decrease or yarnover, work the sts in St st.

· ·

For this lace pattern, the first yarnover and the ssk of each repeat form one companion pair, and the k2tog and second yarnover of each repeat form the other companion pair.

Tank

Lower Body

With larger cir needle, CO 234 (252, 270, 288, 306, 324, 342, 360, 378, 396) sts. Place marker (pm) and join, being careful not to twist sts.

Purl 1 rnd. Knit 1 rnd.

Beg with Rnd 1, work the 9-st rep of Vine Lace in rnds patt 26 (28, 30, 32, 34, 36, 38, 40, 42, 44) times around. *Note:* You may wish to separate each rep with a marker until the patt becomes established.

Work Rnds 2–4 of patt, then rep Rnds 1–4 of patt 26 (27, 28, 29, 30, 31, 32, 33, 34, 35) more times, ending with Rnd 4—108 (112, 116, 120, 124, 128, 132, 136, 140, 144) patt rnds completed; piece measures about 12¾ (13¼, 13¾, 14¼, 14¾, 15¼, 15¾, 16¼, 16½, 17)" (32.5 [33.5, 35, 36, 37.5, 38.5, 40, 41.5, 42, 43] cm) from beg, including the CO and the first 2 rnds before patt began.

Divide Front and Back

NEXT RND: (Rnd 1 of patt) Keeping patt as established, k101 (110, 117, 126, 133, 142, 149, 158, 165, 174) sts for back, BO next 16 (16, 18, 18, 20, 20, 22, 22, 24, 24) sts for left underarm, k101 (110, 117, 126, 133, 142, 149, 158, 165, 174) sts for front and place these sts on holder, BO next 16 (16, 18, 18, 20, 20, 22, 22, 24, 24) sts for right underarm. The first back st will be on the right needle after binding off last underarm st; count this st as the first st of the next row.

Back

Work back sts only in Vine Lace in rows.

Work Row 2 of patt (RS) across back sts, maintaining patt as established (see Note).

SHAPE ARMHOLES

Cont in Vine Lace in rows patt as established, BO 3 (4, 5, 6, 7, 8, 9, 10, 11, 12) sts of next 2 rows (patt Rows 3 and 4), then BO 1 (2, 3, 4, 5, 6, 7, 8, 9, 10) st(s) at beg of foll 2 rows (patt Rows 1 and 2)—93 (98, 101, 106, 109, 114, 117, 122, 125, 130) sts rem.

Purl 1 row (WS; patt Row 3).

NEXT ROW: (RS; patt Row 4) Dec 1 st each end of needle as foll: K1, k2tog, work in patt to last 3 sts, ssk, k1—2 sts dec'd.

Purl 1 row (WS, patt Row 1).

Mark the center 9 (10, 11, 14, 15, 18, 19, 20, 21, 22) sts for center back neck.

NEXT ROW: (RS; patt Row 2 of patt) K1, k2tog, work in patt to marked center sts, join new ball of yarn and BO marked center 9 (10, 11, 14, 15, 18, 19, 20, 21, 22) sts, work in patt to last 3 sts, ssk, k1—40 (42, 43, 44, 45, 46, 47, 49, 50, 52) sts each side.

Working each side separately in patt as established, dec 1 st at each armhole edge as before every RS row 5 times, and *at the same time* at each neck edge BO 10 (11, 11, 11, 11, 12, 12, 12, 12, 12) sts once, then BO 6 sts once, then BO 4 sts once, then BO 3 sts 2 times—9 (10, 11, 12, 13, 14, 14, 16, 17, 19) sts rem each side.

Dec 1 st at each neck edge every RS row 6 (7, 8, 9, 10, 11, 11, 13, 14, 16) times—3 sts rem each side for all sizes; armholes measure about 3½ (3¾, 4, 4¼, 4½, 4¾, 4¾44, 5¼, 5½, 6)" (9 [9.5, 10, 11, 11.5, 12, 12, 13.5, 14, 15] cm). BO all sts.

Front
Replace 101 (110, 117, 126, 133, 142, 149, 158, 165, 174) held front sts on larger cir needle. Rejoin yarn with RS facing, ready to work a RS row. Work as for back.

Finishing
Armhole Edging and Strap
*With crochet hook, ch 36 (see Glossary for crochet instructions). Set aside.

With smaller needles, RS facing, and beg at the selvedge of the 3 sts BO for left back, pick up and knit (see Glossary) 68 (76, 84, 92, 100, 108, 116, 124, 132, 140) sts along armhole opening to the edge of the 3 sts BO for left front, then pick up and knit 33 sts in the bumps at back of crochet chain for left strap—101 (109, 117, 125, 133, 141, 149, 157, 165, 173) sts total. Pm and join for working in the rnd, being careful not to twist sts.

Purl 1 rnd, knit 1 rnd.

NEXT RND: K23 (27, 31, 35, 39, 43, 47, 51, 55, 59), [k2tog, k3] 4 times, k2tog, knit to end—5 sts dec'd; 96 (104, 112, 120, 128, 136, 144, 152, 160, 168) sts rem.

Knit 1 rnd.

PICOT TURNING RND: *K2tog, yo; rep from * to end.

Knit 1 rnd.

NEXT RND: K23 (27, 31, 35, 39, 43, 47, 51, 55, 59), [M1 (see Glossary), k4] 4 times, M1, knit to end—5 sts inc'd; 101 (109, 117, 125, 133, 141, 149, 157, 165, 173) sts.

Knit 2 rnds.

With smaller needle, BO 20 sts, then use the larger needle and the suspended method (see page 56) to BO the next 28 (32, 36, 40, 44, 48, 52, 56, 60, 64) sts loosely and evenly, then use smaller needle and standard method to BO rem sts.

Rep from * for other armhole edging/strap, beg the armhole pick-up at the top of the right front.

Neck Edging
With smaller needles, RS facing, and beg at the top of the left back, *pick up and knit 79 (84, 87, 92, 95, 100, 103, 108, 111, 116) sts along back neck, then pick up and knit 32 sts from base of provisional CO for strap ("unzipping" the crochet chain to expose the loops); rep from * across front neck and base of provisional CO for other strap—222 (232, 238, 248, 254, 264, 270, 280, 286, 296) sts total. Pm and join.

Purl 1 rnd, knit 3 rnds.

PICOT TURNING RND: *K2tog, yo; rep from * to end.

Knit 4 rnds. BO all sts.

Fold neck and armhole edging along picot rnd and, with yarn threaded on a tapestry needle, loosely sew BO edges to WS. Weave in loose ends. Block to measurements.

VICTORIA TANK

Fairy Tale
SCARF

Sarah Swett
Interweave Knits, SPRING 2000

Weaver Sarah Swett spent a lot of time swatching lace patterns in order to find just the right one for a tapestry project and resolved, once she was done, to knit something "real" using her favorite pattern. The scarf begins with an invisible cast-on and a small strip of border. The finished scarf is lovely and delicate, just right for a fairy-tale princess.

FINISHED SIZE

About 13" (33 cm) wide and 90" (229 cm) long, blocked.

YARN

Laceweight (Lace #0).

SHOWN HERE: JaggerSpun Zephyr 2/18 (50% silk, 50% Merino; 5,040 yd [4,608 m]/lb): #M0328 vanilla, 2 oz (55 g).

NEEDLES

U.S. size 4 (3.5 mm). Adjust needle size if necessary to obtain the correct gauge.

NOTIONS

Markers (m); tapestry needle.

GAUGE

20 sts and 30 rows = 4" (10 cm), blocked.

Scarf

Bottom Border

Using a provisional method (see Glossary), CO 11 sts. Purl 1 row.

Beg with Row 1 of Border chart, work 5 complete repeats of the pattern (slipping the first st of every odd-numbered [RS] row and purling all even-numbered [WS] rows), ending with Row 20—5 points knitted. Do not turn.

BODY SET-UP ROW: (WS) Place marker (pm) on needle, pick up and purl (see Glossary) every other slipped loop 6 times, every slipped loop 24 times, then every other slipped loop 7 times (37 picked-up sts; 48 sts total), pm, carefully remove waste yarn from provisional CO and place 11 live sts onto second needle. With WS still facing, set up right border on these 11 sts as foll: P2, yo, ssp, p1, [yo, p2tog] 2 times, yo, p2.

Scarf Body

Beg with Row 1, work Body chart a total of 23 times, ending with Row 20 (WS), and stopping before the right border (do not work the last 11 sts)—piece should measure about 72" (183 cm) before blocking.

Top Border

Turn work. With RS facing, k37 center sts, work Row 1 of Border chart to end.

Work 5 repeats (points) of Border chart, joining the border to the scarf body as foll: Purl the last border st tog with the adjacent center patt st every other WS row (every 4th row) 6 times, every WS row (every other row) 24 times, then every other WS row 7 times, ending with Row 19 of chart. All center patt sts have been joined to the edging—11 sts rem on each border. **Note:** This gives one extra knit row bet rows of lace. If this imperfection bothers you, break the yarn before working the last knit row of the right border (after purling Row 19) and rejoin it at the m to work the last rows of the center and left border patts.

Finishing

With yarn threaded on a tapestry needle and using the Kitchener st (see Glossary), graft the border sts tog. Weave in loose ends, following the line of knitting wherever possible. Wash and block.

Legend

- ☐ k on RS; p on WS
- ◲ ssk on RS; ssp on WS
- ◿ k2tog on RS; p2tog on WS
- ◲ yo
- ☑ sl 1 with yarn in back
- ◿ k3tog on RS; p3tog on WS
- 人 RS: sl 1 kwise, k2tog, psso; WS: p2tog, put st on left needle, pass next st over worked st, return worked st to right needle
- • marker
- ▨ WS rows

Border

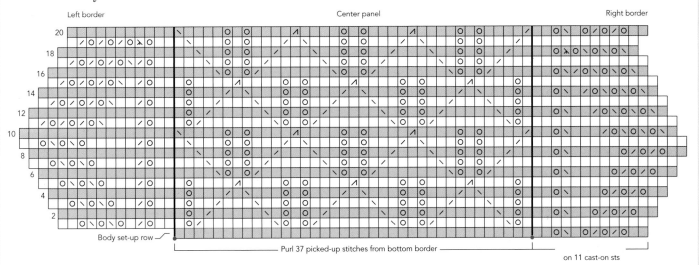

Set-up row   Cast-on row

17
13
9
5
1

Note: WS rows not shown in chart; purl all WS rows.

Body

Left border   Center panel   Right border

20
18
16
14
12
10
8
6
4
2

Body set-up row

Purl 37 picked-up stitches from bottom border

on 11 cast-on sts

Spiral Boot
SOCKS

Véronik Avery
Interweave Knits, SUMMER 2007

Véronik Avery likes lace, especially patterns that are more graphic than fussy. A bold diagonal stitch pattern spirals around the leg of these long socks, topped with a more delicate edging meant to peek out over the top of your boots. Avery incorporates the socks' shaping into the stitch pattern, creating uninterrupted lines.

FINISHED SIZE
8" (20.5 cm) foot circumference and 8¾" (22 cm) long; 11" (28 cm) circumference at top of leg. To fit woman's U.S. shoe size 8.

YARN
Fingering weight (Super Fine #1).

SHOWN HERE: Reynolds Great American Yarns Soft Sea Wool (100% wool; 162 yd [148 m]/50 g): #915 soft pink, 3 skeins. Yarn distributed by JCA.

NEEDLES
U.S. size 2 (2.75 mm): set of 5 double-pointed (dpn). Adjust needle size if necessary to obtain the correct gauge.

NOTIONS
Removable marker (m); tapestry needle.

GAUGE
28 sts and 44 rnds = 4" (10 cm) in St st.

STITCH GUIDE

Calf Spiral Pattern: (multiple of 8 sts)

RND 1: *Knit to last st of needle, transfer last st to next needle without knitting it (it will be worked as the first st of the next needle); rep from * for each needle.

RND 2: *K2tog, k2, yo, k4; rep from * to end.

DEC RND 1: *Knit to last 2 sts of needle, transfer last 2 sts to next needle without knitting them; rep from * for each needle.

DEC RND 2: *K3tog, k2, yo, k3; rep from * to end.

Leg Spiral Pattern: (multiple of 7 sts)

RND 1: *Knit to last st of needle, transfer last st to next needle without knitting it; rep from * for each needle.

RND 2: *K2tog, k2, yo, k3; rep from * to end.

DEC RND 1: *Knit to last 2 sts of needle, transfer last 2 sts to next needle without knitting them; rep from * for each needle.

DEC RND 2: *K3tog, k2, yo, k2; rep from * to end.

Ankle Spiral Pattern: (multiple of 6 sts)

RND 1: *Knit to last st of needle, transfer last st to next needle without knitting it; rep from * for each needle.

RND 2: *K2tog, k2, yo, k2; rep from * to end.

NOTES

While sock appears to use one pattern throughout, it is actually composed of four stitch patterns—three for the leg and one for the foot. The first three patterns progressively narrow the calf to the ankle and travel around the leg, while the last is a flat version to be worked over the instep.

Pattern shifts one stitch to the right on every other round. Ensure that the stitch count on each needle remains constant and that each needle contains whole repeats. In order to keep track of the beginning of the round, place a removable marker on first knit "column" and move it up every few inches.

knit

k2tog

ssk

sl 2 as if to k2tog, k1, p2sso

yo

M1 (see Glossary)

pattern repeat

Cuff

Instep

Sock

Cuff

CO 80 sts. Arrange sts on 4 dpn as foll: 16 sts on Needles 1 and 3, 24 sts each on Needles 2 and 4. Place marker (pm) and join for working in the rnd, being careful not to twist sts.

Knit 1 rnd.

NEXT RND: *K1, yo, k2, sl 1, k2tog, psso, k2, yo; rep from * to end.

Rep last 2 rnds once more.

Purl 2 rnds. Knit 2 rnds.

Work Rows 1–9 of Cuff chart once.

Knit 3 rnds.

Spiral Leg

Work Rnds 1 and 2 of Calf Spiral Patt (see Stitch Guide) 15 times, then work Dec Rnds 1 and 2 of Calf Spiral Patt once—70 sts rem.

Work Rnds 1 and 2 of Leg Spiral Patt 20 times, then work Dec rnds 1 and 2 of Leg Spiral Patt once—60 sts rem.

Work Rnds 1 and 2 of Ankle Spiral Patt until leg measures 12¼" (31 cm) from CO, ending with Rnd 2. Knit 1 rnd.

Heel

HEEL FLAP

Slip sts from Needle 2 to Needle 1—30 sts on Needle 1. Working back and forth on these 30 sts only, work heel flap as foll:

ROW 1: (RS) Sl 1 with yarn in back (wyb), knit to end.

ROW 2: (WS) Sl 1 with yarn in front (wyf), purl to end.

ROW 3: *Sl 1 wyb, k1; rep from * to end.

ROW 4: Sl 1 wyf, purl to end.

Rep Rows 3 and 4 twelve more times—28 rows completed.

TURN HEEL

ROW 1: (RS) Sl 1, k16, ssk, k1, turn.

ROW 2: (WS) Sl 1, p5, p2tog, p1, turn.

ROW 3: Sl 1, knit to 1 st before gap, ssk, k1, turn.

ROW 4: Sl 1, purl to 1 st before gap, p2tog, p1, turn.

Rep Rows 3 and 4 four more times—18 heel sts rem.

SHAPE GUSSET

Pick up sts and renumber needles as foll: (RS) Needle 1: sl 1, k17 heel sts, pick up and knit (see Glossary) 14 sts along the side of the heel flap, pick up and knit 1 st from the row below the first instep st to prevent a hole; Needles 2 and 3: work 30 sts according to Instep chart, placing 15 sts on each needle; Needle 4: pick up and knit 1 st from the row below the last instep st to prevent a hole, then pick up and knit 14 sts along the side of the heel flap, then knit the first 9 sts of Needle 1 onto Needle 4—78 sts: 24 sts on Needle 1, 15 sts on each of Needles 2 and 3, 24 sts on Needle 4. Pm for beg of rnd.

DEC RND: Needle 1: knit to last 2 sts, k2tog; Needles 2 and 3: work all sts in patt; Needle 4: ssk, knit to end—2 sts dec'd.

Work 1 rnd even.

Rep last 2 rnds 8 more times—60 sts rem; 15 sts on each needle.

Foot

Work even in patt until foot measures 6¾" (17 cm) from back of heel, or 2" (5 cm) less than total desired foot length. Knit 4 rnds.

Shape Toe

RND 1: *Needle 1: knit to last 3 sts, k2tog, k1; Needle 2: k1, ssk, knit to end; rep from * for Needles 3 and 4—4 sts dec'd.

RND 2: Knit.

Rep Rnds 1 and 2 six more times—32 sts rem.

Rep Rnd 1 four more times—16 sts rem.

K4 on Needle 1. Break yarn, leaving an 8" (20.5 cm) tail.

Finishing

Slip sts from Needle 4 to Needle 1 and from Needle 2 to Needle 3. Holding Needle 1 and Needle 3 parallel, graft sts using Kitchener st (see Glossary). Weave in loose ends.

Forest Path
STOLE

FINISHED SIZE
About 30" (76 cm) wide and 85" (216 cm) long, blocked.

YARN
Laceweight (Lace #0).

SHOWN HERE: Suri Elegance (100% Suri alpaca; 875 yd [800 m]/100 g): #0100 white house, 3 skeins (2 skeins for a shawl 71" [180 cm] long). Yarn distributed by America's Alpaca.

NEEDLES
U.S. size 3 (3.25 mm): 24" (60 cm) circular (cir) and set of 2 double pointed (dpn). Adjust needle size if necessary to obtain the correct gauge.

NOTIONS
Markers (m); stitch holders; crewel embroidery needle with large eye and blunt point; tailor's wax (available at fabric stores); nylon cord for blocking.

GAUGE
19 sts and 24 rows = 4" (10 cm) in seed stitch, blocked.

Faina Letoutchaia
Interweave Knits, SUMMER 2003

Faina Letoutchaia drew upon the lace-knitting traditions of her Russian homeland and of the Shetland Islands, variations on stitch patterns from Barbara Walker's stitch guides, and a fascination with entrelac to create this elegant alpaca stole. Each of the three lace patterns—fern, birch leaves, and lily of the valley—is worked in its own entrelac unit, which means keeping track of only one lace pattern at a time.

NOTES

To prevent excessive handling of the yarn, place stitches for sections not being worked on holders and use double-pointed needles to work only the required stitches. Transfer stitches not being worked onto holders as each unit is completed.

....

Each entrelac lace unit begins and ends with a row of 20 sts, but the stitch count may change on other rows, depending on the pattern. Each chart shows the center 18 stitches of the entrelac unit. Selvedge sts are not shown on the charts; work them according to the instructions given for each tier.

Stole

Lower Border

With cir needle and using the knitted method (see page 55), CO 141 sts. Do not join. Slipping the first st of every row purlwise (pwise) with yarn in front (wyf) and knitting the last st, work seed st for 20 rows. On next row, place markers (pm) as foll: Sl 1, work 14 sts in seed st, pm, [work 22 sts in seed st, pm] 2 times, work 23 sts in seed st, pm, [work 22 sts in seed st, pm] 2 times, work 14 sts in seed st, k1.

NEXT ROW: (RS) Sl 1, work 14 sts in seed st, then place the last 15 sts worked onto a holder for right border, remove m, [k6, k2tog, k6, k2tog, k6, slip marker (sl m)] 2 times, [k6, k2tog] 2 times, k5, k2tog, sl m, [k6, k2tog, k6, k2tog, k6, sl m] 2 times, place the last 15 sts onto a holder for left border, turn work—100 sts; 20 sts each in 5 marked sections.

Base Triangles

FIRST TRIANGLE

ROW 1: (WS) Sl 1 pwise with yarn in front (wyf), p1—2 sts on right needle. Turn.

ROW 2: Sl 1 kwise with yarn in back (wyb), k1. Turn.

ROW 3: Sl 1 pwise wyf, M1 (see Glossary), p2tog—3 sts. Turn.

ROW 4: Sl 1 kwise wyb, k2. Turn.

ROW 5: Sl 1 pwise wyf, M1, k1, p2tog—4 sts. Turn.

ROW 6: Sl 1 kwise wyb, k1, p1, k1. Turn.

ROW 7: Sl 1 pwise wyf, M1, p1, k1, p2tog—5 sts. Turn.

ROW 8: Sl 1 kwise wyb, k1, p1, k2. Turn.

Cont in this manner, working all odd-numbered (WS) rows as foll: Sl 1 pwise wyf, M1, work in seed st to last st before gap, p2tog, turn; and working all even-numbered (RS) rows as foll: Sl 1 kwise wyb, work in seed st to last st, k1, turn. When all 20 sts in this section have been worked, ending with a WS row, remove m between sections. Do not break yarn.

SECOND, THIRD, FOURTH, AND FIFTH TRIANGLES

With WS facing and beg with first 2 sts of next section, work second triangle same as the first. Rep for third, fourth, and fifth triangles—5 triangles of 20 sts each. If desired, place sts of first, second, third, and fourth triangles on holders. Do not break yarn. Turn.

Right Side Triangle

ROW 1: (RS) Sl 1 pwise wyf, M1—2 sts on right needle for right side triangle; 19 sts on left needle for base triangle or lace unit. Turn.

ROWS 2 AND 4: Sl 1 pwise wyf, k1. Turn.

ROW 3: Sl 1 pwise wyf, ssk. Turn.

ROW 5: Sl 1 pwise wyf, M1, ssk—3 sts on right needle for right side triangle; 17 sts on left needle for base triangle or lace unit. Turn.

ROW 6: Sl 1 pwise wyf, k2. Turn.

ROW 7: Sl 1 pwise wyf, M1, k1, ssk—4 sts on right needle for right side triangle; 16 sts on left needle for base triangle or lace unit. Turn.

ROW 8: Sl 1 pwise wyf, p1, k2. Turn.

ROW 9: Sl 1 pwise wyf, M1, k1, p1, ssk—5 sts on right needle for right side triangle; 15 sts on left needle for base triangle or lace unit. Turn.

Cont in this manner, working all odd-numbered RS rows as foll: Sl 1 pwise wyf, M1, work in seed st to last st before gap, ssk, turn; and working all even-numbered WS rows as foll: Sl 1 pwise wyf, work in seed st to last st, k1, turn. Cont until all 20 sts from base triangle or lace unit have been consumed, ending with a RS row. If desired, place 20 sts for right side triangle on a holder. Do not break yarn.

Tier 1 and All Odd-Numbered Tiers

(Worked from right to left) Pick up sts along selvedge of next base triangle or next lace unit as foll: With RS facing and yarn in front, insert tip of right needle from back to front under both legs of slipped selvedge st, wrap yarn around needle as if to purl, and pull up a loop. Pick up and knit 18 sts along selvedge of a base triangle, or 20 sts along selvedge of a lace unit, in this manner. *Note:* All charts are located on pages 76–77.

SET-UP ROW: (WS) Sl 1 pwise wyf, purl to end, k1, and *at the same time*, if you began with 18 sts, inc 2 sts evenly spaced—20 sts.

For each lace unit, work Rows 1–39 of lace patt from chart, following illustration on page 77 for placement of lace pattern units. *At the same time*, work the lace patt selvedge sts for odd-numbered tiers as foll: On RS: Work first st as sl 1 pwise wyf, and work last st as ssk (to join the last st with first st of unit from previous tier); on WS: Work first st as sl 1 pwise wyf, and work last st as k1. If you have placed non-working sts on holders, transfer live sts to dpn as necessary to join the units. When all units of an odd-numbered tier have been completed, end having just worked Row 39 (RS) of the last lace unit. Do not break yarn.

Left Side Triangle

With RS facing, pick up and knit 20 sts along selvedge of base triangle or lace unit according to the method used for Tier 1.

ROW 1: (WS) Sl 1 pwise wyf, work seed st to last st, k1. Turn.

ROW 2: Sl 1 pwise wyf, work seed st to last 2 sts, k2tog—19 sts rem.

Rep Rows 1 and 2 until 1 st rem, ending with Row 2. Turn. Do not break yarn.

Tier 2 and All Even-Numbered Tiers

(Worked from left to right) Pick up and knit 20 sts along selvedge of left side triangle or next lace unit as foll: With WS facing, insert tip of right needle from front to back under both legs of selvedge st, wrap yarn around needle as if to knit, and pull up a loop—21 sts for first lace unit of the tier (includes 1 st left on needle from left side triangle); 20 sts for all other units in this tier. Turn. For the first lace unit of tier only, dec 1 st in Row 1 of lace patt to eliminate extra st from left side triangle—20 sts.

Work Rows 1–40 of each lace unit in patt according to charts, following illustration for placement of lace pattern units. *At the same time*, work the lace patt selvedge sts for even-numbered tiers as foll: On RS: Work first st as sl 1 kwise wyb and work the last st as k1; on WS: Work first st as sl 1 pwise wyf and work the last st as p2tog (to join last st with first st of unit from previous tier). Place sts for completed units on holders, if desired. When all units for an even-numbered tier have been completed, end having just worked Row 40 (WS) of the last lace unit. Do not break yarn.

Work a right side triangle, then cont with next odd-numbered tier. Cont in this manner until 23 tiers have been completed. Work a left side triangle—1 st rem on needle from left side triangle. *Note:* If you would prefer a shorter shawl, work 21 or 19 tiers, making sure to end with an odd-numbered tier; every pair of tiers removed will reduce the length of the shawl by about 7" (18 cm).

Top Triangles

(Worked from left to right) With WS facing, pick up and knit 20 sts along selvedge of last left side triangle according to directions for even-numbered tiers—21 sts (includes 1 st on needle after completing the previous triangle).

ROW 1: (RS) Sl 1 kwise wyb, work seed st to last st, k1. Turn.

ROW 2: Sl 1 pwise wyf, work seed st to last st, p2tog (to join last st with first st of unit from previous tier). Turn.

ROW 3: Sl 1 kwise wyb, work seed st to last 2 sts, k2tog. Turn.

Rep Rows 2 and 3 until 1 st rem, ending with Row 3. Turn. With WS facing, pick up 20 sts (as for even-numbered tiers) along selvedge of next lace unit—21 sts. Work as for previous top triangle. Cont working top triangles in this manner, joining the final top triangle to live sts of the last right side triangle. Break yarn.

Right Border

Transfer 15 held sts for right border onto a dpn. With WS facing, join new yarn, and maintaining seed st as established, work 14 sts in seed st, end k1.

NEXT ROW: (RS) Sl 1 pwise wyf, work seed st to end. Work border while joining it to side of shawl as foll:

ROW 1: (WS) Wyf, insert right needle tip from back to front under both legs of slipped selvedge st, wrap yarn around needle as if to purl, and pull through a 12"–18" (30.5–45.5 cm) loop. Examine the loop to identify which end is anchored to the work and which end is connected to the yarn supply. Using the anchored end, work in seed st to last st, end k1. Turn.

ROW 2: Using the yarn from the same loop, sl 1 pwise wyf, work seed st to end. Gently pull the end of the loop connected to the yarn supply until excess yarn from loop disappears, and tighten last st.

Pulling up a new long loop every Row 1, rep Rows 1 and 2 until you reach the top of the last right side triangle, ending with Row 2. There are 20 slipped selvedge sts on the side of every triangle, so there should be about 40 rows of seed st border for every triangle. Adjust the pick-up if necessary to make a smooth join with no gaps; the appearance of the join is more important than the actual number of rows. Place 15 sts for right border on a holder. Break off yarn.

Left Border

Transfer 15 held sts for left border onto a dpn. With RS facing, join new yarn and maintaining seed st patt as established, work 14 seed sts, end k1. Turn.

NEXT ROW: (WS) Sl 1 pwise wyf, work seed st to end of row. Work border while joining it to the side of shawl as foll:

ROW 1: (RS) Wyb, insert right needle tip from front to back under both legs of slipped selvedge st, wrap yarn around needle as if to knit, and pull through a 12"–18" (30.5–40.5 cm) loop. Using the anchored end of loop as for right border, work in seed st to last st, end k1. Turn.

ROW 2: Using the yarn from the same loop, sl 1 pwise wyf, work seed st to end. Gently pull the end of loop connected to yarn supply until excess yarn from loop disappears and tighten last st.

Pulling up a new long loop every Row 1, rep Rows 1 and 2 until you reach the top of the last left side triangle, ending with Row 2. Do not break yarn.

Top Border

Transfer left border sts to cir needle with WS facing. Pick up and knit 20 sts along selvedge edge of each top triangle as foll: With yarn in back, insert tip of right needle from front to back under both legs of top triangle slipped selvedge st, wrap yarn around needle as if to knit, and pull up a loop. Transfer held sts for right border to dpn and work in established seed st to last st, end k1—130 sts. Turn.

NEXT ROW: (RS) Sl 1 pwise wyf, work 14 sts of right border in seed st, k100 sts picked up bet borders and *at the same time*, inc 11 sts evenly spaced along picked-up sts, work 14 sts of left border, end k1—141 sts.

Working seed st and selvedges as established, work 21 rows. Cut yarn, leaving a tail about 4 times the width of the knitting stretched to its fullest.

Finishing

To strengthen the yarn for working the sewn bind-off, pass the long tail of yarn through tailor's wax, refreshing the wax several times as you work. Thread tail on crewel embroidery needle and use the sewn method (see page 57) to loosely BO all sts. Weave in loose ends.

Block

Weave a fine, smooth nylon cord in and out along the side selvedges and along the top and bottom edges, leaving 20"–30" (51–76 cm) loops of cord at each corner to allow for stretching the shawl. Wash in lukewarm water with gentle shampoo and rinse in water of the same temperature. Squeeze gently to remove water, and roll in a towel to further remove excess water. Stretch on a large flat surface, pulling on the nylon cord to stretch, and pin the cord in place. Allow to air-dry completely.

☐ k on RS; p on WS	╲ ssk	⋔ sl 2 sts tog kwise, k1, p2sso
⊡ p on RS; k on WS	◯ yo	⋉ sl 1 kwise, k2tog, psso
╱ k2tog	⊼ k3tog	⧟ ([k1tbl, yo] 2 times, k1tbl) in same st
		⑤ p5tog
		M M1 (make 1; see glossary)
		▨ no stitch

Fern

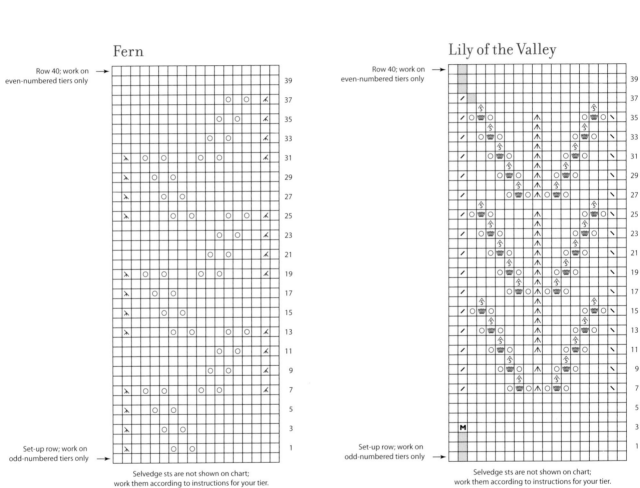

Row 40; work on even-numbered tiers only →

Set-up row; work on odd-numbered tiers only →

Selvedge sts are not shown on chart;
work them according to instructions for your tier.

Lily of the Valley

Row 40; work on even-numbered tiers only →

Set-up row; work on odd-numbered tiers only →

Selvedge sts are not shown on chart;
work them according to instructions for your tier.

Birch Leaves

Row 40; work on
even-numbered tiers only →

Set-up row; work on
odd-numbered tiers only →

39

37

35

33

31

29

27

25

23

21

19

17

15

13

11

9

7

5

3

1

Selvedge sts are not shown on chart;
work them according to instructions for your tier.

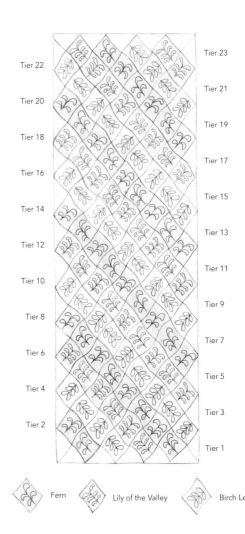

Tier 23

Tier 22

Tier 21

Tier 20

Tier 19

Tier 18

Tier 17

Tier 16

Tier 15

Tier 14

Tier 13

Tier 12

Tier 11

Tier 10

Tier 9

Tier 8

Tier 7

Tier 6

Tier 5

Tier 4

Tier 3

Tier 2

Tier 1

Fern   Lily of the Valley   Birch Leaves

FINISHED SIZE

31½ (35½, 39½, 43½, 47½, 51½)" (80 [90, 100.5, 110.5, 120.5, 131] cm) bust circumference. Sweater shown measures 35½" (90 cm), worn with minimal positive ease.

YARN

Fingering weight (Super Fine #1).

SHOWN HERE: Rowan Cashcotton 4 ply (35% cotton, 25% polyamide, 18% angora, 13% viscose, 9% cashmere; 197 yd [180 m]/50 g): #917 citron, 7 (8, 8, 9, 10, 11) skeins. *Note: This yarn has been discontinued; try substituting Rowan Cashsoft 4 ply, Rowan Purewool 4 ply, Rowan Organic Cotton 4 ply, or Rowan Siena.*

NEEDLES

BODY AND SLEEVES: U.S. size 3 (3.25 mm): 24" (60 cm) circular (cir). NECKBAND AND HOOD: U.S. size 2 (2.75 mm): 24" (60 cm) cir. Adjust needle size if necessary to obtain the correct gauge.

NOTIONS

Stitch holders; waste yarn for provisional CO; tapestry needle.

GAUGE

26 sts and 36 rows = 4" (10 cm) in St st on larger needle; 24 sts and 37 rows = 4" (10 cm) in lace patt on larger needle.

Après Surf HOODIE

Connie Chang Chinchio
Interweave Knits, SUMMER 2008

This casual but classic pullover brings a little edge to delicate lace by setting an allover arrowhead lace motif into a frame of wide stockinette bands and raw edges. A wide crossover neckband flows seamlessly into a neat, tidy edging for the lace hood. Connie Chang Chinchio uses shaping and set-in sleeves to keep the look feminine and a luxurious yarn for a seasonless garment.

NOTES

Knit the first and last stitch of every row for selvedge stitches. Work all increases and decreases inside the selvedge stitches.

....

When decreasing for neck and armhole shaping in lace pattern, make sure that each pattern decrease (ssk or k2tog) is accompanied by a corresponding increase (yo) and that each double decrease (sl 1, k2tog, psso) is accompanied by two increases (yo); otherwise, work these stitches in stockinette stitch.

....

When working the I-cord BO over a larger area (e.g., the body hems or the neckband), sssk rather than ssk every 5th st to avoid puckering.

Hoodie

Back

With larger needle and using the invisible provisional method (see Glossary), CO 105 (117, 131, 143, 157, 169) sts. Do not join.

Work in St st (knit on RS; purl on WS) until piece measures 3 (3, 3, 3, 3½, 3½)" (7.5 [7.5, 7.5, 7.5, 9, 9] cm) from CO, ending with a WS row.

SHAPE WAIST

NEXT ROW: (RS row) K1, ssk, knit to last 3 sts, k2tog—2 sts dec'd.

Work 7 rows even.

Rep last 8 rows 5 more times, and *at the same time* when piece measures 4½ (4½, 4½, 4½, 5, 5)" (11.5 [11.5, 11.5, 11.5, 12.5, 12.5] cm) from CO and second row of waist decs are complete, on a WS row, dec 8 (8, 10, 10, 12, 12) sts evenly spaced across—93 (105, 117, 129, 141, 153) sts rem.

Beg lace section on next RS row as foll: Work 2 (4, 2, 4, 2, 4) sts in St st, work Lace chart to last 2 (4, 2, 4, 2, 4) sts, work 2 (4, 2, 4, 2, 4) sts in St st.

Cont in patt until all waist decs are complete—85 (97, 109, 121, 133, 145) sts rem.

Work even in lace patt until piece measures 9¾ (9¾, 9¾, 9¾, 10¼, 10¼)" (25.5 [25.5, 25.5, 25.5, 26, 26] cm) from CO, ending with a WS row.

SHAPE BUST

NEXT ROW: (RS) K1, M1, work in patt to last st, M1, k1—2 sts inc'd.

Work 9 rows even in patt.

Rep last 10 rows 4 more times—95 (107, 119, 131, 143, 155) sts.

Work even in lace patt until piece measures 15½ (15½, 15½, 15¾, 16¼, 16½)" (39.5 [39.5, 39.5, 40, 41.5, 42] cm) from CO, ending with a WS row.

Lace

		O	⋏	O			9
	O	╱		╲	O		7
O	╱				╲	O	5
╱		O		O		╲	3
╱		O		O		╲	1

Legend:
- ☐ k on RS; p on WS
- O yo
- ╱ k2tog
- ╲ ssk
- ⋏ sl 1, k2tog, psso
- ☐ pattern repeat

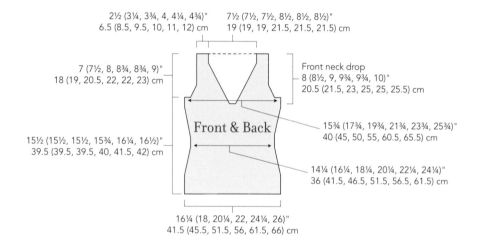

Front & Back

2½ (3¼, 3¾, 4, 4¼, 4¾)"
6.5 (8.5, 9.5, 10, 11, 12) cm

7½ (7½, 7½, 8½, 8½, 8½)"
19 (19, 19, 21.5, 21.5, 21.5) cm

7 (7½, 8, 8¾, 8¾, 9)"
18 (19, 20.5, 22, 22, 23) cm

Front neck drop
8 (8½, 9, 9¾, 9¾, 10)"
20.5 (21.5, 23, 25, 25, 25.5) cm

15¾ (17¾, 19¾, 21¾, 23¾, 25¾)"
40 (45, 50, 55, 60.5, 65.5) cm

15½ (15½, 15½, 15¾, 16¼, 16½)"
39.5 (39.5, 39.5, 40, 41.5, 42) cm

14¼ (16¼, 18¼, 20¼, 22¼, 24¼)"
36 (41.5, 46.5, 51.5, 56.5, 61.5) cm

16¼ (18, 20¼, 22, 24¼, 26)"
41.5 (45.5, 51.5, 56, 61.5, 66) cm

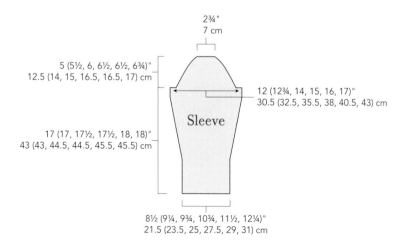

Sleeve

2¾"
7 cm

5 (5½, 6, 6½, 6½, 6¾)"
12.5 (14, 15, 16.5, 16.5, 17) cm

12 (12¾, 14, 15, 16, 17)"
30.5 (32.5, 35.5, 38, 40.5, 43) cm

17 (17, 17½, 17½, 18, 18)"
43 (43, 44.5, 44.5, 45.5, 45.5) cm

8½ (9¼, 9¾, 10¾, 11½, 12¼)"
21.5 (23.5, 25, 27.5, 29, 31) cm

SHAPE ARMHOLES

BO 5 (6, 7, 5, 6, 7) sts at beg of next 2 rows, then 0 (0, 0, 3, 4, 5) sts at beg of foll 0 (0, 0, 2, 2, 2) rows—85 (95, 105, 115, 123, 131) sts rem.

Dec 1 st each end of needle every RS row 5 (6, 7, 8, 10, 11) times—75 (83, 91, 99, 103, 109) sts rem.

Work even in patt until armholes measure 7 (7½, 8, 8¾, 8¾, 9)" (18 [19, 20.5, 22, 22, 23] cm), ending with a WS row.

Place 15 (19, 23, 24, 26, 29) sts on a holder for right shoulder, 45 (45, 45, 51, 51, 51) sts on a holder for back neck, and 15 (19, 23, 24, 26, 29) sts on a holder for left shoulder.

Front

Work as for back until bust shaping is complete.

Work even in patt until piece measures 14½ (14½, 14½, 14¾, 15¼, 15½)" (37 [37, 37, 37.5, 38.5, 39.5] cm) from CO, ending with a WS row.

DIVIDE FOR NECK

Cont in lace patt, work 44 (50, 56, 62, 68, 74) sts, join new yarn, BO 7 sts, work to end of row—44 (50, 56, 62, 68, 74) sts each side.

Working each side separately, dec 1 st in patt at each neck edge every 14th row 4 times, and *at the same time* when piece measures 15½ (15½, 15½, 15¾, 16¼, 16½)" (39.5 [39.5, 39.5, 40, 41.5, 42] cm) from CO, shape armholes as for back—30 (34, 38, 42, 44, 47) sts rem each side after all shaping is complete.

Work even in patt until armholes measure 7 (7½, 8, 8¾, 8¾, 9)" (18 [19, 20.5, 22, 22, 23] cm), ending with a WS row. Place 15 (19, 23, 24, 26, 29) sts from each armhole edge on holders for shoulders and 15 (15, 15, 18, 18, 18) sts from each neck edge on holders for hood.

Sleeves

With larger needle, use the provisional method to CO 56 (60, 64, 70, 74, 80) sts. Work in St st until piece measures 5½ (5½, 5½, 5½, 6, 6)" (14 [14, 14, 14, 15, 15] cm) from CO, ending with a RS row.

NEXT ROW: (WS; dec row) Dec 2 (2, 2, 4, 4, 4) sts evenly spaced across row—54 (58, 62, 66, 70, 76) sts rem.

NEXT ROW: Work 2 (4, 2, 4, 2, 1) sts in St st, work Lace chart to last 3 (5, 3, 5, 3, 2) sts, work 3 (5, 3, 5, 3, 2) sts in St st.

Inc 1 st as M1 1 st from each end of needle every 12th row 6 (6, 0, 0, 0, 0) times, then every 10th row 3 (3, 7, 4, 1, 1) time(s), then every 8th row 0 (0, 4, 8, 12, 12) times, working new sts into lace patt—72 (76, 84, 90, 96, 102) sts.

Work even in patt until piece measures 17 (17, 17½, 17½, 18, 18)" (43 [43, 44.5, 44.5, 45.5, 45.5] cm) from CO, ending with a WS row.

SHAPE CAP

BO 5 (6, 7, 5, 6, 7) sts at beg of next 2 rows, then 0 (0, 0, 3, 4, 5) sts at beg of foll 0 (0, 0, 2, 2, 2) rows—62 (64, 70, 74, 76, 78) sts rem.

Dec 1 st in patt each end of needle every row 3 (3, 3, 3, 3, 5) times, then every other row 4 (4, 6, 7, 7, 8) times—48 (50, 52, 54, 56, 52) sts rem.

Dec 1 st each end of needle every 4th row 5 (6, 6, 5, 5, 5) times, then every other row 3 (3, 4, 6, 6, 5) times, then every row 3 (3, 3, 3, 4, 3) times—26 sts rem.

BO 2 sts at beg of next 2 rows, then 3 sts at beg of foll 2 rows—16 sts rem.

BO all sts.

Finishing

Block pieces to measurements. Remove provisional CO from front, placing live sts on larger needle. BO all sts using the I-cord BO (see Glossary). Rep BO for back and sleeves.

Join shoulders using the three-needle BO (see Glossary). Sew in sleeves, easing any fullness at top. Sew sleeve and side seams.

Hood

With smaller needle, RS facing, and beg at right-front neck edge, work 15 (15, 15, 18, 18, 18) sts from right-front neck holder in lace patt, pick up and knit 3 (3, 3, 5, 5, 5) sts at right shoulder seam, work 45 (45, 45, 51, 51, 51) sts from back neck holder in lace patt, pick up and knit 3 (3, 3, 5, 5, 5) sts at left-shoulder seam, and work 15 (15, 15, 18, 18, 18) sts from left-front neck holder in lace patt—81 (81, 81, 97, 97, 97) sts.

Working all sts in lace patt, inc 1 st each end of needle every 12 (12, 12, 14, 14, 14)th row 7 (7, 7, 6, 6, 6) times, working new sts into lace patt—95 (95, 95, 109, 109, 109) sts.

Work even until hood measures 12¼" (31 cm) from pick-up, ending with a WS row.

SHAPE TOP OF HOOD

K47 (47, 47, 54, 54, 54), BO 1 st, knit to end—47 (47, 47, 54, 54, 54) sts rem each side.

Work left side of hood first, working short-rows (see Glossary) as foll, while keeping in patt:

NEXT ROW: (WS) Work to last 5 (5, 5, 6, 6, 6) sts, wrap & turn (w&t), turn, work to end of row.

NEXT ROW: (WS) Work to last 10 (10, 10, 12, 12, 12) sts, w&t, work to end of row.

NEXT ROW: (WS) Work to last 16 (16, 16, 18, 18, 18) sts, w&t, work to end of row.

NEXT ROW: (WS) Work to last 22 (22, 22, 25, 25, 25) sts, w&t, work to end of row.

NEXT ROW: (WS) Work to last 28 (28, 28, 33, 33, 33) sts, w&t, work to end of row.

NEXT ROW: (WS) Work across all sts, picking up and working wraps as you come to them—47 (47, 47, 54, 54, 54) sts. Place sts on holder.

With WS facing, join yarn to right side of hood. Work 1 WS row in patt. Work short-rows as for left side of hood, beg each short-row with RS facing and ending with WS facing.

With RS tog, use the three-needle BO to join left and right sides of hood.

Neckband

With smaller needle and RS facing, beg at base of neck, pick up and knit 54 (57, 60, 65, 65, 67) sts along right-front edge, 184 sts along hood edge, and 54 (57, 60, 65, 65, 67) sts along left-front edge—292 (298, 304, 314, 314, 318) sts total.

NEXT ROW: (WS) Purl.

Working in St st, inc 1 st as M1 1 st from each end of needle every RS row 3 times—298 (304, 310, 320, 320, 324) sts.

Work even in St st until band measures 1½" (3.8 cm), ending with a WS row. BO all sts using the I-cord BO. Sew edge of left-front band to BO sts at neck opening. Sew right-front band over left-front band to BO sts at neck opening.

Weave in loose ends. Block sweater again if desired.

Luminarie
SKIRT

Annie Modesitt
Interweave Knits, SUMMER 2009

FINISHED SIZE

$32^{1}/_{2}$ ($35^{3}/_{4}$, 39, $42^{1}/_{4}$, $45^{1}/_{2}$)" (82.5 [90.5, 99, 107.5, 115.5] cm) waist circumference and 25" (63.5 cm) long (all sizes). Skirt shown measures 39" (99 cm) waist.

YARN

Sportweight (Fine #2).

SHOWN HERE: Blue Moon Fiber Arts Luscious Silk (100% silk; 360 yd [329 m]/127 g): spinel, 4 (4, 4, 4, 5) skeins.

NEEDLES

U.S. size 6 (4 mm): 24" (60 cm) or longer circular (cir). Adjust needle size if necessary to obtain the correct gauge.

NOTIONS

Markers (m); tapestry needle; size I/9 (5.5 mm) crochet hook; waste yarn (optional).

GAUGE

20 sts and 28 rows = 4" (10 cm) in St st; 11-st Tier 1 block = $2^{1}/_{2}$" (6.5 cm) wide and 3" (7.5 cm) high.

Airy lace panels cascade in entrelac tiers in Annie Modesitt's Luminarie Skirt. Working in the round, with shaping built into panels that grow larger toward the hem, yields a gentle, flattering A-line silhouette. The simplicity of the arrow motif combines with the movement created by entrelac squares to create a deceptively complex-looking garment.

NOTES

To make the piece easier to look at as you work, place the stitches of each block onto a strand of waste yarn. Use a different color of waste yarn for each tier, making it easier to tell when to begin a new tier.

··

Circumference of finished skirt at lower edge measures 75 (82½, 90, 97½, 105)" (190.5 [209.5, 228.5, 247.5, 266.5] cm).

Skirt

CO 110 (120, 130, 140, 150) sts. Place marker (pm) and join in the rnd.

RND 1: Purl.

RND 2: *K2, sl 2 as if to k2tog, k1, p2sso, k3, yo, k1, yo, k1; rep from * around.

Rep Rnds 1 and 2 two more times.

NEXT RND: Purl, inc 0 (1, 2, 3, 4) st(s) evenly spaced around—110 (121, 132, 143, 154) sts.

Base Triangles

(11-st WS triangles) Turn work so WS is facing.

ROW 1: (WS) P2, turn.

ROW 2: (RS) K2, turn.

ROW 3: P3, turn.

ROW 4: K3, turn.

ROW 5: P4, turn.

ROW 6: K4, turn.

ROW 7: Purl to 1 st past last turning point, turn.

ROW 8: Knit to end, turn.

Rep last 2 rows 5 more times—10 triangle sts.

ROW 19: P11, do not turn—11-st triangle complete.

Rep Rows 1–19 of base triangle 9 (10, 11, 12, 13) more times—10 (11, 12, 13, 14) 11-st triangles.

Tier 1

(11-st RS blocks) Turn work so RS is facing. K11.

BLOCK
ROW 1: (RS) Pick up and knit (see Glossary) 11 sts along side of base triangle.

ROW 2: (WS) Sl 1, p10, turn.

ROW 3: [Ssk (see Glossary), yo] 5 times, ssk (last st of block tog with first st of base triangle).

Rep Rows 2 and 3 ten more times—all sts of base triangle have been worked tog with this block.

Rep block instructions 9 (10, 11, 12, 13) more times—10 (11, 12, 13, 14) 11-st blocks.

Tier 2
(11-st WS blocks) Turn work so WS is facing. P11.

BLOCK
ROW 1: (WS) Pick up and purl (see Glossary) 11 sts along side of Tier 1 block.

ROW 2: (RS) Sl 1, [yo, k2tog] 5 times.

ROW 3: (WS) P10, p2tog (last st of block tog with first st of Tier 1 block).

Rep Rows 2 and 3 ten more times—all sts of Tier 1 block have been worked tog with this block. Rep block instructions 9 (10, 11, 12, 13) more times—10 (11, 12, 13, 14) 11-st blocks.

Tier 3
(13-st RS blocks) Turn work so RS is facing. K11.

BLOCK
ROW 1: (RS) Pick up and knit 13 sts evenly spaced along side of Tier 2 block.

ROW 2 AND ALL WS ROWS: Sl 1, p12, turn.

ROW 3: (RS) K1, yo, ssk, k3, yo, ssk, k2, k2tog, yo, ssk (last st of block tog with first st of Tier 2 block).

ROW 5: K1, yo, ssk, k1, k2tog, yo, k1, yo, ssk, k1, k2tog, yo, ssk (last st of block tog with first st of Tier 2 block).

ROW 7: K1, yo, ssk, k2tog, yo, k3, yo, ssk, k2tog, yo, ssk (last st of block tog with first st of Tier 2 block).

Rep Rows 2–7 two more times, then work Rows 2–5 once more—all sts of Tier 2 block have been worked tog with this block.

Rep block instructions 9 (10, 11, 12, 13) more times—10 (11, 12, 13, 14) 13-st blocks.

Tier 4
(13-st WS blocks) Turn work so WS is facing. P13.

BLOCK
ROW 1: (WS) Pick up and purl 13 sts along side of Tier 3 block.

ROW 2: (RS) Sl 1, yo, ssk, k3, yo, ssk, k2, k2tog, yo, k1.

ROW 3 AND ALL WS ROWS: P12, p2tog (last st of block tog with first st of Tier 3 block).

ROW 4: Sl 1, yo, ssk, k1, k2tog, yo, k1, yo, ssk, k1, k2tog, yo, k1.

ROW 6: Sl 1, yo, ssk, k2tog, yo, k3, yo, ssk, k2tog, yo, k1.

ROW 7: P12, p2tog (last st of block tog with first st of Tier 3 block).

Rep Rows 2–7 three more times, then work Rows 2 and 3 once more—all sts of Tier 3 block have been worked tog with this block.

Rep block instructions 9 (10, 11, 12, 13) more times—10 (11, 12, 13, 14) 13-st blocks.

Tier 5
(15-st RS blocks) Turn work so RS is facing. K13.

BLOCK
ROW 1: (RS) Pick up and knit 15 sts evenly spaced along side of Tier 4 block.

ROW 2 AND ALL WS ROWS: Sl 1, p14, turn.

ROW 3: (RS) K2tog, yo, k1, yo, ssk, k3, yo, ssk, k2, k2tog, yo, ssk (last st of block tog with first st of Tier 4 block).

ROW 5: K2tog, yo, k1, yo, ssk, k1, k2tog, yo, k1, yo, ssk, k1, k2tog, yo, ssk (last st of block tog with first st of Tier 4 block).

ROW 7: K2tog, yo, k1, yo, ssk, k2tog, yo, k3, yo, ssk, k2tog, yo, ssk (last st of block tog with first st of Tier 4 block).

Rep Rows 2–7 three more times, then work Rows 2 and 3 once more—all sts of Tier 4 block have been worked tog with this block.

Rep block instructions 9 (10, 11, 12, 13) more times—10 (11, 12, 13, 14) 15-st blocks.

Tier 6
(15-st WS blocks) Turn work so WS is facing. P15.

BLOCK
ROW 1: (WS) Pick up and purl 15 sts along side of Tier 5 block.

ROW 2: (RS) Sl 1, yo, ssk, k3, yo, ssk, k2, k2tog, yo, k1, yo, ssk.

ROW 3 AND ALL WS ROWS: P14, p2tog (last st of block tog with first st of Tier 5 block).

ROW 4: Sl 1, yo, ssk, k1, k2tog, yo, k1, yo, ssk, k1, k2tog, yo, k1, yo, ssk.

ROW 6: Sl 1, yo, ssk, k2tog, yo, k3, yo, ssk, k2tog, yo, k1, yo, ssk.

ROW 7: P14, p2tog (last st of block tog with first st of Tier 5 block).

Rep Rows 2–7 four more times—all sts of Tier 5 block have been worked tog with this block.

Rep block instructions 9 (10, 11, 12, 13) more times—10 (11, 12, 13, 14) 15-st blocks.

Tier 7
(17-st RS blocks) Turn work so RS is facing. K15.

BLOCK
ROW 1: (RS) Pick up and knit 17 sts evenly spaced along side of Tier 6 block.

ROW 2 AND ALL WS ROWS: Sl 1, p16, turn.

ROW 3: (RS) K2tog, yo, k1, yo, ssk, k3, yo, ssk, k2, k2tog, yo, k1, yo, sssk (last 2 sts of block tog with first st of Tier 6 block).

ROW 5: K2tog, yo, k1, yo, ssk, k1, k2tog, yo, k1, yo, ssk, k1, k2tog, yo, k1, yo, sssk (last 2 sts of block tog with first st of Tier 6 block).

ROW 7: K2tog, yo, k1, yo, ssk, k2tog, yo, k3, yo, ssk, k2tog, yo, k1, yo, sssk (last 2 sts of block tog with first st of Tier 6 block).

Rep Rows 2–7 four more times—all sts of Tier 6 block have been worked tog with this block.

Rep block instructions 9 (10, 11, 12, 13) more times—10 (11, 12, 13, 14) 17-st blocks.

Garter Triangles
Cont working with RS facing.

FIRST TRIANGLE
ROW 1: (RS) Pick up and knit 16 sts along side of Tier 7 block—33 sts total for triangle.

ROW 2: (WS) K33.

ROW 3: Ssk, k15, pm, ssk, turn—31 sts rem for triangle.

ROW 4: Sl 1, knit to end.

ROW 5: Ssk, knit to m, ssk, turn—2 sts dec'd.

ROW 6: Sl 1, knit to end.

Rep Rows 5 and 6 thirteen more times—3 sts rem.

NEXT ROW: (RS) Sl 2 as if to k2tog, remove m, k1, p2sso—1 st rem. Fasten off last st as foll: Pull on st to elongate it, pull ball of yarn through st, then pull to tighten st.

SECOND TRIANGLE
With RS facing, k17, then pick up and knit 16 sts along side of Tier 7 block—33 sts total for triangle. Beg with Row 2, work as for first triangle.

NEXT TRIANGLES

Rep second triangle instructions 8 (9, 10, 11, 12) more times—10 (11, 12, 13, 14) garter triangles.

Finishing

Note: See Glossary for crochet instructions. With crochet hook, join yarn to hem edge at beg of a garter triangle. *[Ch 3, sl st in hem edge] 16 times along edge of garter triangle; rep from * 9 (10, 11, 12, 13) more times—160 (176, 192, 208, 224) ch-3 sps.

NEXT RND: *Ch 4, sl st into next ch-sp; rep from * around.

Rep last rnd once more. Fasten off. Weave in loose ends. Steam block.

Make a 40–60" (101.5–152.5 cm) twisted cord (see Glossary) and run through the eyelets at the top edge of skirt.

LUMINARIE SKIRT

Facing Lilies
STOLE

FINISHED SIZE
29" (73.5 cm) wide and 68" (172.5 cm) long, after blocking.

YARN
Laceweight (Lace #0).

SHOWN HERE: Wooly West Horizons (100% wool; 525 yd [480 m]/50 g): natural, 2 skeins.

NEEDLES
CENTER: size 3 (3.25 mm): 10" (25.5 cm) straight (bamboo or wood recommended). LACE EDGE: size 3 (3.25 mm): 32" (80 cm) circular (cir; bamboo or wood recommended). Adjust needle size if necessary to obtain the correct gauge.

NOTIONS
Markers (m; 3 in one color and 1 different); tapestry needle; size G/6 (4 mm) crochet hook; 4 yd cotton waste yarn.

GAUGE
18 sts and 28 rows = 4" (10 cm) in St st, before blocking.

Nancy Bush
Interweave Knits, SPRING 2010

Nancy Bush modifies a traditional Estonian lace pattern called "Lily of the Valley and Stones" for the ground of this stole. Graphic eyelet diamonds—created with chained decreases and yarnovers—alternate with yarnovers forced into a graceful curve by the adjacent lines of decreases. The contemporary edging is knitted directly onto the completed center, unlike the traditional edge, which is knit separately and sewn onto the center.

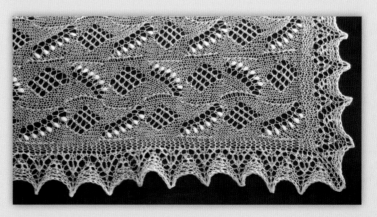

Slipping Edge Stitches

Sl first st of each row of the center section as if to purl, then bring the working yarn to the back between the needles, then cont in patt.

......

Nupp ("button" or "knob" in Estonian)

The nupps in this shawl are made up of 7 sts. Very loosely work (k1, yo, k1, yo, k1, yo, k1) all in same st—1 st inc'd to 7 sts. On the foll row, p7tog—7 nupp sts dec'd to 1 st again.

......

Picking Up Selvedge Stitches

Pick up and knit sts at a ratio of 3 sts for every 2 chain selvedge sts as foll: Pick up 1 st under both loops of the first selvedge st, then pick up 1 st under just the back loop of the 2nd selvedge st, then pick up 1 st under both loops of the 2nd selvedge st—3 sts picked up from 2 selvedge sts.

NOTES

The center section of the shawl is framed in garter st, with 8 garter rows (4 garter ridges) at each end and 4 garter sts at each side; the garter frame is not shown on the chart.

......

The odd-numbered chart rnds have a yo at the end of each side, just before the marker; take care that these yo's remain to the right of the marker; do not allow the marker to "migrate" underneath the yo's.

Stole

Center Section

With cotton waste yarn and crochet hook, work a crochet chain (see Glossary) about 100 sts long. Place a knot in the tail as you complete the chain, so you can find it later. With straight needles and working yarn, pick up and knit (see Glossary) 92 sts from the underside of the chain.

Knit 8 rows, always slipping the first st of every row (see Stitch Guide), and placing same-color markers (pm) 4 sts in from each end on the last row—84 sts between m; 4 sts outside m at each side.

Slipping the first st of each row and keeping edge sts at each side in garter st, work Rows 1–32 of Lily and Stone chart 12 times, then work Rows 33–46 once—398 chart rows total.

Knit 8 rows, slipping the first st of each row as before, and ending with a WS row—414 rows total; 207 chain selvedge sts at each side. Leave sts on needle.

Lace Edge

With cir needle, knit across all sts, inc 10 sts evenly, pm—102 sts. With RS still facing, pick up 2 sts in first selvedge st (see Stitch Guide), pick up and knit 153 sts from next 102 selvedge sts (3 sts for every 2 selvedge sts), pick up 2 sts in next selvedge st, pick up and knit 153 sts from next 102 selvedge sts, pick up 2 sts in last selvedge st, pm—312 sts picked up from long edge of shawl. Beg at the knotted end of the waste yarn, carefully undo the crochet chain, placing the live sts on a needle. Knit across these 92 sts, inc 10 sts evenly, pm—102 sts along short end of shawl. Pick up and knit 312 sts along 2nd long edge, pm of contrasting color for beg of rnd—828 sts total. *Note:* The first st after each m is a corner st; do not remove these m until edge is complete.

Purl 1 rnd.

Establish patt from Rnd 1 of Lace Edge chart as foll: Sl m, **k1 (corner st), yo, *k1, yo, [sl 1, k2tog, psso], yo, k3, yo, k3tog, yo; rep from * to 1 st before next m, k1, yo, sl m; rep from ** 3 more times for rem 3 sides—8 sts inc'd; 1 st at each end of all 4 sides.

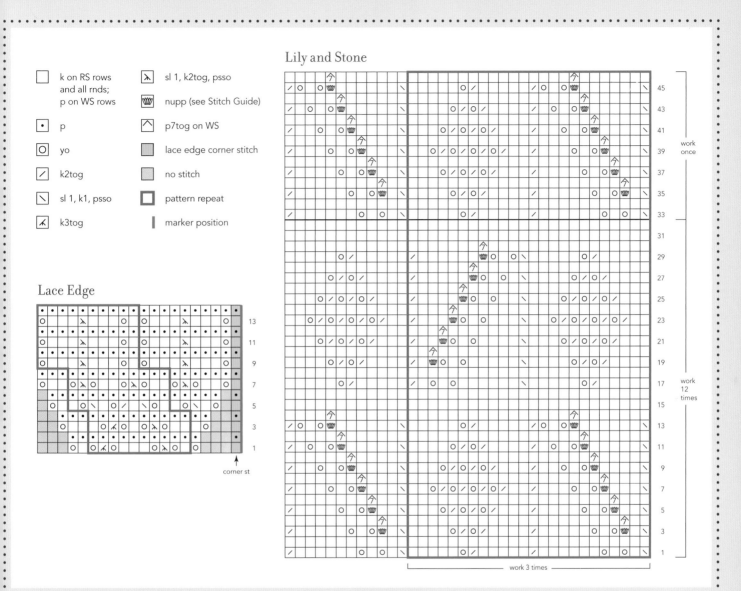

Lily and Stone

Legend

- ☐ k on RS rows and all rnds; p on WS rows
- · p
- ○ yo
- ╱ k2tog
- ╲ sl 1, k1, psso
- ⅄ k3tog
- ⅄ sl 1, k2tog, psso
- ⊞ nupp (see Stitch Guide)
- ⋀ p7tog on WS
- ▨ lace edge corner stitch
- ▨ no stitch
- ☐ pattern repeat
- | marker position

work once

work 12 times

work 3 times

Lace Edge

corner st

Note: Cont in this manner, work Rnds 2–14 of Lace Edge chart—860 sts total; 320 sts along each long side; 110 sts along each short side.

BO all sts using a doubled strand of yarn and the k2tog BO (see Glossary).

Finishing

Wash shawl in warm water and soap. Carefully block shawl to the desired finished measurements, pinning out each [yo, k1, yo] point around the lace edge. Cover with clean towels and allow to dry. Weave in all loose ends.

FINISHED SIZE

TAM: 18 (22)" (45.5 [56] cm) head circumference, to fit a child (woman).

WIDE SCARF: 8" (20.5 cm) wide and 75" (190.5 cm) long, after washing and blocking.

NARROW SCARF: 5" (12.5 cm) wide and 73" (184.5 cm) long, after washing and blocking.

YARN

Laceweight (Lace #0).

SHOWN HERE: Jacques Cartier Clothier Qiviuk (100% qiviut; 217 yd [198 m]/28 g): #4008 maroon: 1 ball for tam, 2 balls for wide scarf, 1 ball for narrow scarf.

NEEDLES

TAM: U.S. size 1 (2.25 mm): 16" (40 cm) circular (cir); size 2 (2.75 mm): 16" (40 cm) cir and set of 4 or 5 double-pointed (dpn). SCARVES: size 3 (3.25 mm). Adjust needle size if necessary to obtain the correct gauge.

NOTIONS

Markers (m); elastic thread (for tam; optional); stitch holder (narrow scarf only); tapestry needle.

GAUGE

TAM: 26 sts and 38 rows = 4" (10 cm) in tam top patt on larger needle, before washing and blocking; 26 sts and 34 rows = 4" (10 cm) after washing and blocking. SCARVES: 23 sts and 40 rows = 4" (10 cm) in acre patt, before washing and blocking; 20 sts and 26 rows = 4" (10 cm) after washing and blocking.

Qiviuk Webs
TAM & SCARF

Gayle Roehm

Interweave Knits, HOLIDAY GIFTS 2007

The open gauge and lace stitches in this winter set make a little precious fiber go a long way. Inspired by the yarn, which she found as light and airy as a spider's web, Gayle Roehm created a lacy design for the tam that mimics the slightly irregular look of a web and incorporated Shetland web and spider motifs into the scarf.

NOTES

The tam requires a very loose cast-on so the lower edge will be elastic. Try a knitted cast-on or a backward-loop cast-on (see page 55).

....

The wide scarf is worked in garter stitch lace in one piece, beginning with the lower edging. After working lace patterns and the long center section, the lace patterns are worked again. Then the upper edging is knitted onto the remaining scarf stitches.

....

The narrow scarf only requires one ball of the recommended yarn. To allow you to use every inch of the precious qiviut, you'll knit the first end of the scarf with its lace patterns, put this section on a holder, then knit the other end, followed by the long stretch of acre patterning. When you have a yard or two left, graft the first end onto the scarf in progress.

Tam

CO 112 (144) sts very loosely (see Note). Place marker (pm) and join for working in the rnd, being careful not to twist sts. With smaller cir needle, work rib as foll:

RND 1: *K2, p2; rep from * around.

Rep Rnd 1 until rib measures 1½" (3.8 cm) from CO (about 18 rnds). Change to larger needle.

INC RND 1: [K1 through back loop (tbl), M1P (see Glossary), p6 (8), pm] 16 times—128 (160) sts.

RNDS 2–4: *K1tbl, p7 (9); rep from * around.

INC RND 2: *K1tbl, M1P, purl to m; rep from * around—16 sts inc'd.

NEXT RND: *K1tbl, purl to m; rep from * around.

Rep last rnd 2 more times. Rep last 4 rnds 4 (3) more times—208 (224) sts total, 12 (13) purl sts between m. Work 4 rnds even in patt.

Spiders

RND 1: *Sl 1 pwise, p3, work Row 1 of Tam Spider chart, p2 (3); rep from * around.

RND 2: *K1tbl, p3, work Row 2 of Tam Spider chart, p2 (3); rep from * around.

Cont in this manner, slipping the knit sts every other rnd, until 6 rows of Tam Spider chart are complete.

CHILD'S SIZE ONLY

RND 7: *Sl 1 pwise, purl to m; rep from * around.

RND 8: *K1tbl, purl to m; rep from * around.

RND 9: Rep Rnd 7.

BOTH SIZES

Beg with Rnd 6 (1) of chart, work through Rnd 47 of Tam Top chart, working decs as indicated and changing to dpn when necessary—8 sts rem. Break yarn, thread tail through rem sts, and fasten off.

Tam

☐	k on RS; p on WS
℞	k1tbl
⋁	sl 1
•	p on RS; k on WS
⁄	k2tog
⼃	k3tog
⧵	ssk
⤡	p2tog on RS; k2tog on WS
⤢	p3tog on RS; k3tog on WS
O	yo
☐	pattern repeat

Top

Spider

Wide Scarf

Lower Edging

CO 6 sts. Knit 1 row.

Work Rows 1–2 of Edging chart, then rep Rows 3–18 of chart 5 times. BO 6 sts, leaving last st on right needle—you are at top right corner of straight edge.

With right needle, pick up and knit 1 st in each garter ridge along the straight edge—41 sts total. Knit 1 row.

EYELET ROW 1: (RS) K1, *yo, k2tog; rep from * across.

Knit 5 rows.

Small Spiders

K3, work Row 1 of Small Spider chart 5 times, k3. Work through Row 6 of chart, keeping first and last 3 sts in garter st. Knit 4 rows, dec 1 st on last row—40 sts rem.

Lace Holes

Work Rows 1–6 of Lace Holes chart. Knit 4 rows.

Large Spider Webs

K5, work Row 1 of Large Spider Web chart 3 times, k5. Work through Row 14 of chart, keeping first and last 5 sts in garter st, and working Row 4 as foll: K4, k2tog, work Row 4 of chart 2 times, then work to last st of chart, k2tog, k5. Knit 4 rows.

EYELET ROW 2: (RS) K1, *yo, k2tog; rep from * to last st, k1.

Knit 1 row.

Acre Pattern

ROW 1: (RS) K6, k2tog, *yo, k2, yo, ssk (see Glossary), k5, k2tog; rep from * once more, yo, k2, yo, ssk, k6.

ROW 2: (WS) Knit.

Cont in Acre patt until scarf measures 60" (152.5 cm), ending with a WS row. Rep Eyelet Row 2. Knit 5 rows.

Work Rows 1–14 of Large Spider Web chart, keeping first and last 5 sts in garter st, and working Row 4 as above. Knit 4 rows.

Work Rows 1–6 of Lace Holes chart. Knit 4 rows, inc 1 st on last row—41 sts.

Work Rows 1–6 of Small Spider chart, keeping first and last 3 sts in garter st. Knit 6 rows. Rep Eyelet Row 1. Knit 1 row.

Upper Edging

(RS) Leaving all sts on needle, use the knitted method (see page 55) to CO 6 sts—47 sts total. Work Rows 1–2 of Edging chart, then work Rows 3–18 of chart 5 times, working each RS row as foll: Work to last st of chart, k2tog (last st of edging and next st of scarf), turn. When all 5 reps of chart have been worked, BO all sts.

Narrow Scarf

Work as for wide scarf, with these changes:

Lower Edging

Work 3 reps of Edging chart. After picking up and knitting in garter ridges, there will be 25 sts total.

Small Spiders

K2, work Row 1 of Small Spider chart 3 times, k2. Work through Row 6 of chart, maintaining 2 garter sts each edge. Knit 4 rows, dec 1 st on last row—24 sts rem.

Large Spider Webs

K2, work Row 1 of Large Spider Web chart 2 times, k2. Work through Row 14 of chart, keeping first and last 2 sts in garter st and working Row 4 as foll: K1, k2tog, work Row 4 of chart once, then work to last st of chart, k2tog, k2. After working Eyelet Row 2, inc 2 sts on next row—26 sts. Break yarn. Place sts on holder.

Work second end as for first, but after last row, do not break yarn.

Scarf

Legend:

- ☐ k on RS; p on WS
- ℞ k1tbl
- ☑ sl 1
- • p on RS; k on WS
- ╱ k2tog
- ╱ k3tog
- ╲ ssk
- ⬈ p2tog on RS; k2tog on WS
- ⬈ p3tog on RS; k3tog on WS
- ○ yo
- ☐ pattern repeat

Edging

Large Spider Web

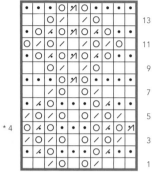

* 4

* work as given in directions

Small Spider

Lace Holes

Acre Pattern

ROW 1: (RS) K5, k2tog, yo, k2, yo, ssk, k4, k2tog, yo, k2, yo, ssk, k5.

ROW 2: (WS) Knit.

Cont in Acre patt until 1–2 yd of yarn rem, ending with a RS row. Do not break yarn; leave sts on needle. With yarn threaded on a tapestry needle, use Kitchener st (see Glossary) to graft sts on needle to held sts. Finish and block as for wide scarf.

Finishing

Weave in loose ends. Soak tam in hot water with a small amount of gentle soap. Rinse, rubbing the pieces in your hands very gently. Roll in a terry towel, squeeze out as much water as possible, and block as follows:

Tam: Stretch over a 10"–12" (25.5–30.5 cm) diameter dinner plate.

Scarves: Block to shape (blocking wires are ideal).

Note: When wet, the qiviut yarn is very limp and stretchy, almost mushy. You'll need to pat the pieces into shape, pushing any ribbing tog, and let them completely air-dry. Put a hand towel over the pieces and give them a few shots with a steam iron or let them dry over a heat vent. Once dry, the pieces will hold their shape. You may want to add some elastic thread around the lower edge of the ribbing of the tam.

Paisley Lace
SHAWL

Evelyn A. Clark
Interweave Knits, SPRING 2005

As with many traditional paisley shawls, this one begins as a simple square panel, worked from the center out and surrounded with an elaborate border that is finished with a picot edging. To make the paisley motifs line up when the shawl is folded in a triangle, the orientation of the motifs is reversed on half of the shawl.

FINISHED SIZE

40" to 48" (101.5 cm to 122 cm) square. Shawl shown was gently blocked to 40" (101.5 cm) square.

YARN

Laceweight (Lace #0).

SHOWN HERE: JaggerSpun Zephyr (50% merino, 50% silk; 5,040 yd [4,608 m]/lb [454 g]): cinnabar, about 1,125 yd (1,028 m) or 3.5 oz (99 g).

NEEDLES

U.S. size 5 (3.75 mm): 16" and 24" (40 and 60 cm) circular (cir) and set of 5 double-pointed (dpn). Adjust needle size if necessary to obtain the correct gauge.

NOTIONS

Size F/5 (3.75 mm) crochet hook; 3 removable markers (m) in one color plus 1 m of a different color; tapestry needle.

GAUGE

20 sts and 40 rows = 4" (10 cm) in garter stitch worked in the round, before blocking.

The first time you work the 8 rounds of the Eyelet chart, you will work the 8-stitch pattern repeat once for each quarter of the shawl; the second time, you will work the 8-stitch repeat twice for each quarter, and so on, until you have worked the required number of rounds.

Shawl
Eyelet and Garter Center

Using a crochet hook, CO 8 sts with Emily Ocker's Circular Beginning (see page 55)—8 sts on hook. Divide sts on 2 double-pointed needles and use different-color m to mark beg of rnd. Purl 1 rnd.

Divide sts evenly on 4 dpns, pulling the beginning yarn tail to tighten the CO sts into a closed circle.

RND 1: *Yo, k1; rep from * to end of rnd—16 sts.

RND 2 AND ALL EVEN-NUMBERED RNDS: Purl.

RND 3: *Yo, k3, yo, k1; rep from * to end of rnd—24 sts.

RND 5: *Yo, k5, yo, k1; rep from * to end of rnd—32 sts.

RND 7: *Yo, k2, k2tog, yo, k3, yo, k1, place marker (pm) for corner st; rep from * to end of rnd, using the different colored marker at the end of the last rep to indicate beg of rnd—40 sts.

RND 9: *Yo, k2, [k2tog, yo] 2 times, k3, yo, k1; rep from * to end of rnd —48 sts.

RND 11: *Yo, k4, k2tog, yo, k5, yo, k1; rep from * to end of rnd—56 sts.

RND 13: *Yo, knit to 1 st before marker, yo, k1; rep from * to end of rnd—64 sts; 16 sts in each quarter.

RND 14: Purl.

Change to Eyelet chart (see Notes), and rep Rnds 1–8 thirteen times—104 Eyelet chart rnds completed; 480 sts; 120 sts in each marked quarter of the shawl.

Eyelet Outline

RND 1: *Yo, knit to 1 st before marker, yo, k1; rep from * to end of rnd—488 sts; 122 sts in each quarter.

RNDS 2, 4, AND 6: Purl.

RND 3: (eyelet outline) *Yo, k1, [yo, k2tog] 60 times, yo, k1; rep from * to end of rnd—496 sts; 124 sts in each quarter.

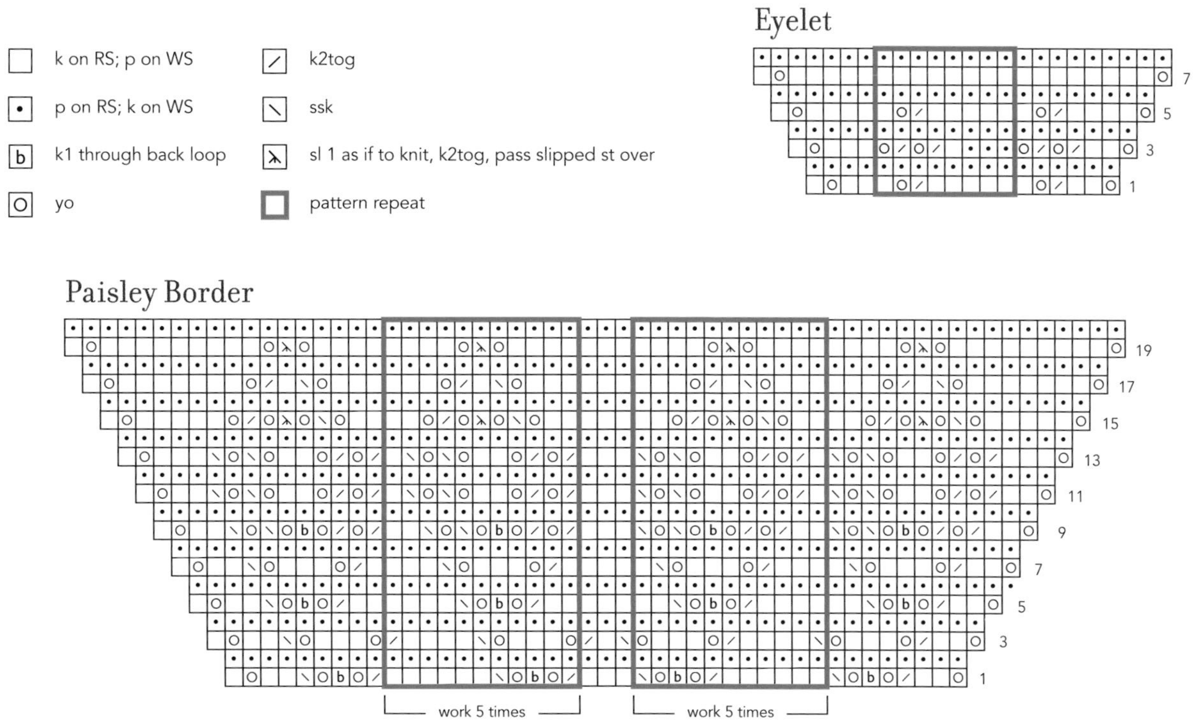

Chart Key

☐	k on RS; p on WS
•	p on RS; k on WS
b	k1 through back loop
O	yo
/	k2tog
\	ssk
⋏	sl 1 as if to knit, k2tog, pass slipped st over
☐	pattern repeat

Eyelet

Paisley Border

work 5 times · work 5 times

RND 5: Rep Rnd 1—504 sts; 126 sts in each quarter.

RND 7: Rep Rnd 1—512 sts; 128 sts in each quarter.

RND 8: Purl.

Paisley Lace Border

Work Rnds 1–20 of Paisley Border chart—592 sts; 148 sts in each quarter.

Work Rnds 1–6 only of Eyelet Outline (above), working [yo, k2tog] 74 times on Rnd 3—616 sts; 154 sts in each quarter.

NEXT RND: *M1 (see Glossary), knit to 1 st before marker, M1, k1; rep from *—624 sts; 156 sts in each quarter.

Picot Edging

Remove markers as you come to them. *Using the knitted method (see page 55), CO 3 new sts onto left needle tip, BO 6 sts (the 3 new sts and next 3 sts from edge of shawl), slip the last st from right needle to left needle; rep from * until all shawl sts have been BO—1 st rem. Cut yarn and pull tail through rem st to fasten off.

Finishing

Soak shawl in water for at least 20 minutes. Roll in towel to remove excess water. Spread out on a flat surface and smooth into shape. The shawl shown was gently stretched out by smoothing and pulling the picots to straighten. If you would like to stretch your shawl larger, you may find it helpful to use blocking wires. Pull out each picot to lengthen; pins are not necessary. Leave in place until thoroughly dry. Weave in loose ends.

PAISLEY LACE SHAWL

Shaping Lace Garments

EUNNY JANG

Adapted from "Beyond the Basics," Interweave Knits, *Fall 2006*

Knitting lace patterns by hand is a satisfying exercise in a world that often moves too fast. The knitting is rhythmic and meditative; the finished project is a tangible expression of tradition and history. In her primer on knitted lace (see pages 6–11), Jackie Erickson-Schweitzer discusses the basics of knitted lace: how yarnovers and decreases are paired to create lace patterns, how to read lace charts, and how to fix mistakes. Shaping a garment instead of a lace motif uses a different but complementary process.

SHAPING LACE PROJECTS

Many lace projects—shawls, stoles, and scarves—require minimal shaping, or none at all. Rectangular scarves and stoles, for example, are knitted straight up from the cast-on edge. After the lace pattern is established, it repeats without interruption. In circular shawls worked from the center out, increases are worked into the pattern repeats, and triangular shawls often use columns of yarnovers (without accompanying decreases) along a center spine and/or along the edges for shaping. In these projects, the basic repeat of the lace pattern remains intact as you knit, and the charts and written instructions spell out where to place the increased stitches and how to work them.

Garments of lace, however, are often shaped with increases and decreases along side seams and bind-offs at armholes. Shaping often cuts into pattern repeats, wreaking havoc with the balance of yarnovers and decreases. Remember that in lace pattern repeats, the number of stitches increased through yarnovers is usually balanced by the number of stitches decreased to maintain a constant stitch count. Adding or removing stitches for shaping purposes interferes with that balance unless the knitter understands the yarnover/decrease structure in the pattern repeat and takes time to plan ahead.

Two methods for shaping will allow you to add and subtract stitches at the edges of your piece while maintaining the correct number of stitches overall. The simplest method is to work any edge stitches that fall before and after the first and last full repeats of the pattern in a plain stitch that matches the background of the lace fabric—usually stockinette stitch. The second, less conspicuous, way to shape lace is to continue the pattern right up to the edge by working partial repeats on either side of the first and last full repeats. Either way, becoming thoroughly familiar with the pattern, anticipating the stitch count on every row, and using a visual guide can all be helpful.

Figure 1

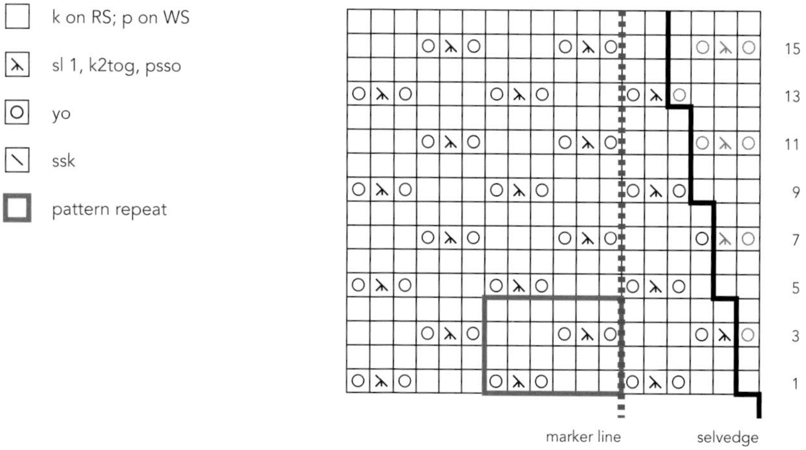

Legend:
- □ k on RS; p on WS
- ⅄ sl 1, k2tog, psso
- ○ yo
- ╲ ssk
- ▢ pattern repeat

(chart showing rows 1, 3, 5, 7, 9, 11, 13, 15 with marker line and selvedge labeled below)

marker line   selvedge

USING A CHART TO PLAN FOR SHAPING

Patterns that provide charts often indicate shaping lines on the grid, but written instructions may not give any clue beyond, "Work X repeats of lace pattern, decreasing 1 stitch at each edge every 4th row 3 times and then increasing 1 stitch at each edge every 2nd row 6 times." Charting the lace pattern and drawing the decreases and increases as they occur will help you to keep the stitch count consistent. On graph paper, chart two or three pattern repeats beginning with the first row of the work, as shown in Figure 1. (You don't need to chart the entire width of your knitting, only enough repeats at either edge to accommodate the number of stitches added or removed by the shaping.) Then draw a line to indicate the shaping and another vertical line to show the beginning of the first full repeat and the end of the last full repeat. In Figure 1, the heavy black line shows the right edge of the knitted piece and a series of decreases worked every four rows, beginning with Row 1. The dotted line indicates the beginning of the first full repeat.

After mapping your lace pattern and adding the marker and shaping lines, compare it to the knitting on your needle. From the right side of the work, divide your stitches in the following way: place two stitch markers, one at the beginning of the first full pattern repeat and one at the end of the last full repeat. If the row begins and ends with a full repeat, place the marker one repeat in (in this example, six stitches) from either edge. You'll have three sections: the shaped right edge of the piece to the right of the first marker, the straight middle of uninterrupted pattern repeats, and the shaped left edge of the piece, to the left of the second marker.

SHAPING WITH DECREASES
Decreasing Stitches in Stockinette Stitch

The simplest way to work decreases in a lace piece is to switch from the lace pattern to plain stitches (usually stockinette) in the areas before and after the markers as soon as it is no longer possible to work a full pattern repeat.

Allover-patterned garments (and some triangular shawls) are often shaped this way. The gauge difference between the solid and openwork sections is usually negligible after blocking. However, if the body pattern is very open and airy, a distinct "stair step" effect will be visible where solid fabric and lace meet.

Whenever the number of stitches between marker and edge is fewer than the number required for the full repeat—in this example, the repeat requires six stitches—simply ignore lace patterning and knit the stitches plain, incorporating any shaping at the extreme edges of the piece. In Figure 2, Row 1 shows the first decrease. (Remember that each square on the chart represents one stitch after the row has been completed.) Work the first six stitches as ssk, k4, work the center section in pattern, and work the last six stitches of the row outside the second marker as k4, k2tog (not shown on the chart)—five stitches remain between each marker and the selvedge. On Rows 2–4 work the five stitches at each side in stockinette as shown in Figure 2.

If, eventually, all the stitches between marker and edge have been eliminated, and there are still decreases to be made, simply reposition the markers at the beginning and end of the first and last full repeats, and continue in the same manner.

Decreasing Stitches in Pattern

If you don't want to interrupt the flow of the lace pattern by working plain stitches at the edges, you can work with partial repeats in a way that maintains the necessary stitch count while keeping the integrity of the pattern. Once you've charted your pattern and have marked off the stitches on your needle to correspond with the sections on the chart as previously explained, focus on the number of stitches between the marker and the edge (the incomplete pattern repeat), noting the relationship of those stitches to the row below, and to the whole repeat. Remember that yarnovers make a new stitch without affecting any stitches from the row below, while decreases reduce two or three stitches from the row below into a single stitch.

According to the chart of the original pattern in Figure 1, there should be five stitches between the marker and edge on Row 3 after working the first decrease in Row 1. Take a look at the work on the needle and imagine each stitch you'll make, going from the marker out to the edge. Following the chart in Figure 1, you can see three plain stitches immediately precede the marker, then a yarnover, and then a double decrease (which eliminates two stitches) to begin the row. If you make a double decrease over the first three stitches and then work a yarnover, you will be left with only four stitches before the marker instead of five, and the pattern will be off by one stitch.

Think of how pattern elements work together in the whole repeat: the double decrease represents an action happening to three stitches from the row below, the stitch to the right of the decrease symbol (which has already been decreased away), the stitch directly below it, and the stitch to the left of it. In order to keep the stitch count correct, the actual work needs to turn two, not three, stitches into one. Figure 3 shows how to work a partial repeat of the pattern in a way that maintains the stitch count. In Row 3, the symbol at the beginning of the row has changed to show a single (ssk) decrease. Count this decrease as the first stitch of the row. Then work yo, k3 to the marker. When you finish the row, five stitches will remain between the marker and the edge.

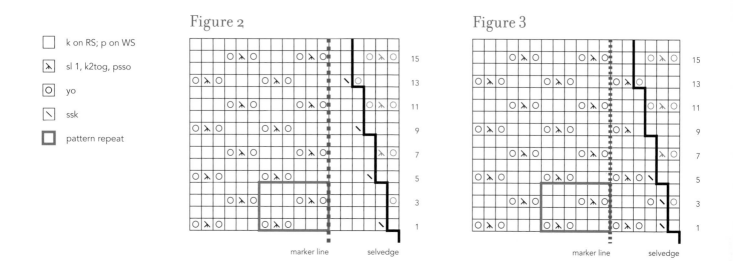

	k on RS; p on WS
	sl 1, k2tog, psso
	yo
	ssk
	pattern repeat

Figure 2

Figure 3

marker line   selvedge

marker line   selvedge

In Figures 1 and 3, the chart shows a shaping decrease at the beginning of Row 5. Work the first two stitches together as ssk and continue in pattern.

According to the original pattern (Figure 1), Row 7 would begin with a yarnover as the first of four stitches between marker and edge. Consider again what the whole pattern repeat looks like—a double decrease and another yarnover originally preceded the remaining yarnover in Row 7. A single yarnover without an accompanying decrease is unbalanced—if worked, it would create a new stitch and increase the stitch count by one. The solution? Simply ignore the yarnover and knit the first stitch of the row to maintain the right number of stitches between marker and edge.

In Rows 9 and 13, each double decrease removes two stitches, and the single yarnover restores one of those two stitches, resulting in a decrease of one stitch. Because both Rows 9 and 13 are decrease rows, simply omitting the yarnover in front of each double decrease, as shown in

Figure 3, will reduce the stitch count by one stitch as the shaping requires.

SHAPING WITH INCREASES
Increasing Stitches in Stockinette Stitch
Stockinette stitch can also be used to work increases along the edge of a sweater body or sleeve. Place markers before and after the first and last full repeats as explained before, and work the stitches between the marker and the edge in stockinette stitch, increasing when shown on the chart and using the increase technique called for in the pattern. If no particular increase technique is spelled out, you can cast on a new stitch at the edge using the backward-loop cast-on (see page 55), or work a make 1 (M1) or raised bar increase (see Glossary) one stitch in from the edge. When enough stitches have been added to work an entire repeat, move the marker to the outside of the new repeat and work the newly introduced edge stitches according to the row of the pattern you're on. (You don't need to wait until Row 1 of the pattern to start working the pattern over the new stitches.)

▢	k on RS; p on WS
⋏	sl 1, k2tog, psso
○	yo
⟍	ssk
▢	pattern repeat

Figure 4

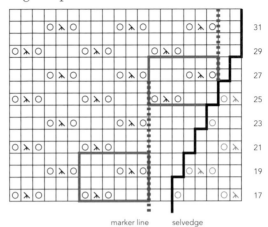

marker line　　selvedge

In the example in Figure 4, one stitch is increased every right-side row, beginning with Row 19. When Row 25 has been completed, there are six stitches between the marker and edge—enough stitches to work a full repeat if you are increasing by casting on a new stitch at the end of the needle. If you are working an increase one stitch in from the selvedge, you'll need to wait until you have seven stitches between marker and selvedge to begin a new repeat. On the next lace pattern row (Row 27 in this example), move the marker to the outside of the new six-stitch repeat and work stockinette between the new marked position and the selvedge as before.

Increasing Stitches in Pattern

You increase stitches in pattern in much the same way that you decrease them.

Plot the pattern, marker, and shaping lines, and first and last full repeats on a chart, as shown in Figure 5 (the

figure shows only the first full repeat). Place markers on your needle before and after the first and last full pattern repeats. Again, focus on the number of stitches between marker and edge and remember that each square on the chart equals one stitch on the needle after the row is completed. In Row 17 of this example, there are two stitches before the first marker. Count stitches from the marker to the edge to decide how to handle the partial repeat. Here, instead of working a double decrease and yarnover as shown in Figure 5, work a single decrease to balance the single yarnover and maintain the stitch count of two as shown in Figure 6. Row 19 is the first increase row, and you can simply increase one stitch to bring the stitch count before the marker to three as shown.

In Row 21, the three stitches of the preceding row need to become four stitches worked, according to the chart and counting back from the marker, as a yarnover, a double decrease, a yarnover, and a plain stitch (the increased

Figure 5

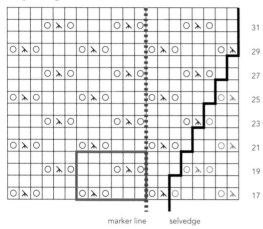

marker line   selvedge

Figure 6

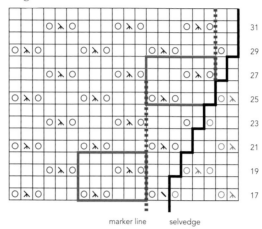

marker line   selvedge

stitch). The yarnovers create a whole new stitch without affecting any from the row below, but the double decrease will reduce all three available stitches of Row 20 into one stitch, leaving nothing to increase from. To solve the problem, cast on one stitch at the edge with a knitted or backward-loop cast-on, knit that stitch as the first stitch of the row, and continue.

In Row 23, the four stitches of the preceding row must become five, but the row as shown in the original chart (Figure 5) starts with the same unbalanced partial repeat that appeared at the beginning of Row 17. Again, count from the marker—three plain stitches precede it, then a yarnover, then a double decrease. Using the principles learned when decreasing, think about how the previous row's stitches will be used in this row—three available stitches can be used for the three plain stitches of Row 23, and the yarnover doesn't require a stitch from the previous row, leaving one stitch for the square containing the double decrease symbol. Of

course, working a double decrease would throw everything off by two stitches. Solution? Work the first stitch plain, work the yarnover required by the pattern without any companion decrease at all to increase to five stitches between the marker and the selvedge, as shown in Figure 6, and continue.

After Row 25, there are six stitches between marker and edge, enough to work a full repeat. On the next lace patterned row, Row 27, move the marker to set off those six stitches as the new first full repeat, and continue.

As you grow more familiar with how lace works, markers will take a back seat to your own ability to read the work and intuitively know what needs to be done. If you understand how the unglamorous building blocks of knitted lace— yarnovers and decreases—work together, then you'll be able to master shaping in the most complex constructions and patterns.

SHAPING LACE GARMENTS

Oriel Lace
BLOUSE

Shirley Paden
Interweave Knits, SUMMER 2007

FINISHED SIZE
36 (40½, 44½, 49)" (91.5 [103, 113, 24.5] cm) bust circumference. Sweater shown measures 36" (91.5 cm).

YARN
Sportweight (Fine #2).

SHOWN HERE: Alchemy Yarns Silken Straw (100% silk; 236 yd [216 m]/40 g): #92W moonstone, 6 (6, 7, 8) skeins.

NEEDLES
U.S. sizes 8 (5 mm), 7 (4.5 mm), 6 (4 mm), 5 (3.75 mm), 3 (3.25 mm), and 2 (2.75 mm). Adjust needle sizes if necessary to obtain the correct gauge.

NOTIONS
Size C/2 (2.75 mm) crochet hook; seven ⅜" (1 cm) buttons; stitch holders; tapestry needle.

GAUGE
22 sts and 32 rows = 4" (20 cm) in patt on size 5 needles after blocking; 1 patt rep = 2¼" (5.5 cm) wide and 3½" (9 cm) high on size 5 needles after blocking.

A gently fitted silhouette and belled sleeves are the perfect foil for an intricate allover lace pattern of interlocking arches. Shirley Paden used a drapey, slightly variegated silk ribbon to keep the top light and airy. She kept the silhouette simple to show off the lace; a high neck and flared sleeves add grace. The close-fitting collar closes up the back with a row of small buttons.

Sloped Bind-Off (used for armholes and sleeve caps)
Do not work the last st of the row before the BO; turn.
On the BO row, slip the first st from the left needle
pwise, then BO the rem st from the previous row over the
slipped st. This technique is used only on the first BO st
of a row.

NOTES

Size 8 needle is used for the cast-on to provide an elastic
edge for the lace pattern.

Row counts are given throughout the instructions because
the neckband is a continuation of the front and back; the
neck pickup begins on a specific row.

Garter stitch selvedges are worked throughout garment;
knit the first and last stitch on all rows.

Alternate working two rows with one skein and two rows with
another to disguise any color differences between skeins.

Front
With largest needles, CO 99 (111, 123, 135) sts. Change to
size 5 needles and purl 1 WS row.

NEXT ROW: (RS) K1 (selvedge st; work in garter st), work 97 (109,
121, 133) sts according to Row 1 of Oriel chart, beg and ending as
indicated for your size, k1 (selvedge st; work in garter st).

Shape Waist
Cont in charted patt, dec 1 st inside selvedge sts each end of
needle every 8th row 6 times, ending with chart Row 20—87
(99, 111, 123) sts rem; piece measures about 6" (15 cm) from CO.

Work 12 rows even in patt, ending with chart Row 4—piece
measures about 7½" (18 cm) from CO.

Shape Bust
NEXT ROW: (RS; inc row) Inc 1 st inside selvedge st each
end of needle—2 sts inc'd.

Cont in patt, rep inc row every 7th row 5 more times, ending with
chart Row 12—99 (111, 123, 135) sts; piece measures about 12"
(30.5 cm) from CO.

 k on RS; p on WS

• p on RS; k on WS

／ k2tog

＼ ssk

○ yo

▢ pattern repeat

Oriel

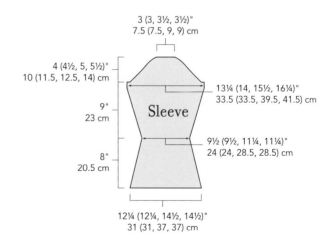

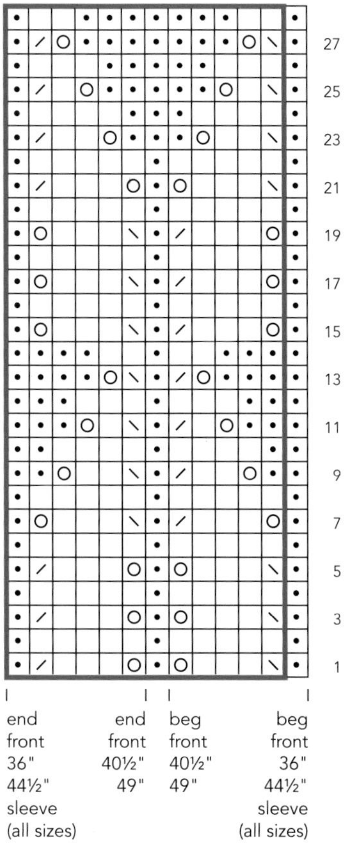

Chart "Oriel" with rows numbered 1–27 (odd).

Bottom labels:
end front 36" 44½" sleeve (all sizes)
end front 40½" 49"
beg front 40½" 49"
beg front 36" 44½" sleeve (all sizes)

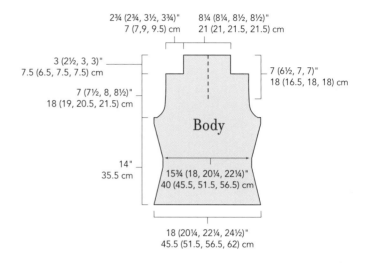

Body

2¾ (2¾, 3½, 3¾)"
7 (7,9, 9.5) cm

8¼ (8¼, 8½, 8½)"
21 (21, 21.5, 21.5) cm

3 (2½, 3, 3)"
7.5 (6.5, 7.5, 7.5) cm

7 (6½, 7, 7)"
18 (16.5, 18, 18) cm

7 (7½, 8, 8½)"
18 (19, 20.5, 21.5) cm

14"
35.5 cm

15¾ (18, 20¼, 22¼)"
40 (45.5, 51.5, 56.5) cm

18 (20¼, 22¼, 24½)"
45.5 (51.5, 56.5, 62) cm

Sleeve

3 (3, 3½, 3½)"
7.5 (7.5, 9, 9) cm

4 (4½, 5, 5½)"
10 (11.5, 12.5, 14) cm

13¼ (14, 15½, 16¼)"
33.5 (33.5, 39.5, 41.5) cm

9"
23 cm

9½ (9½, 11¼, 11¼)"
24 (24, 28.5, 28.5) cm

8"
20.5 cm

12¼ (12¼, 14½, 14½)"
31 (31, 37, 37) cm

Work 16 rows even in patt, ending with chart Row 28—piece measures about 14" (35.5 cm) from CO.

Shape Armholes

Use the sloped BO (see Stitch Guide on page 112) to BO 4 sts at beg of next 2 rows, then 3 sts at beg of foll 2 (4, 4, 6) rows, then 2 sts at beg of foll 2 (6, 6, 8) rows, then 1 st at beg of foll 6 (4, 6, 6) rows—75 (75, 85, 87) sts rem.

Work 44 (44, 46, 46) rows even in patt after last BO row, ending with chart Row 28 (4, 8, 12)—armholes measure about 7 (7½, 8, 8½)" (18 [19, 20.5, 21.5] cm). Place sts on holder.

Back

Work as for front through the armhole shaping, then work 12 (12, 14, 14) rows even in patt after last BO row, ending with chart Row 24 (28, 4, 8)—armholes measure about 3 (3½, 4, 4½)" (7.5 [9, 10, 11.5] cm).

Divide for Placket

NEXT ROW: (RS) Work 38 (38, 43, 44) sts in patt, then place these sts on holder for right back—37 (37, 42, 43) sts rem for left back. With RS facing, knit into front and back of next st (k1f&b), work to end in patt—38 (38, 43, 44) sts.

Work 1 WS row even. At beg of next RS row, create a selvedge st at the placket opening by working k1f&b in the first st—39 (39, 44, 45) sts. Keeping in patt as established and maintaining 1-st garter st selvedge at each edge, work even until armhole measures about 7 (7½, 8, 8½)" (18 [19, 20.5, 21.5] cm), ending with chart Row 28 (4, 8, 12). Place sts on holder.

Right Back

With WS facing, transfer 38 (38, 43, 44) right-back sts to needle and join yarn at placket opening. Work 1 WS row even. Create a selvedge st at placket opening by working k1f&b at end of next RS row—39 (39, 44, 45) sts.

Keeping in patt as established and maintaining 1-st garter st selvedge at each edge, work even until armhole measures about 7 (7½, 8, 8½)" (18 [19, 20.5, 21.5] cm), ending with chart Row 28 (4, 8, 12). Place sts on holder.

Sleeves

With largest needles, CO 63 (63, 75, 75) sts. Change to size 7 needles and purl 1 WS row. Keeping first and last st in garter st for selvedge sts, work center 61 (61, 73, 73) sts according to Oriel chart, working the next 54 rows changing needle sizes as foll: 16 rows with size 7, 16 rows with size 6, 14 rows with size 5, and 8 rows with size 3, ending with chart Row 26— piece measures about 8" (20.5 cm) from CO.

Shape Sleeve

Change to size 5 needles and work as foll: Inc 1 st each end of needle on next row, then every foll 14th (9th, 14th, 9th) row 4 times, then every foll 0 (10th, 0, 10th) row 0 (2, 0, 2) times, ending with chart Row 27—73 (77, 85, 89) sts.

Work 15 rows even in patt, ending with chart Row 14—piece measures about 17" (43 cm) from beg.

Shape Cap

Use the sloped BO to BO 4 sts at beg of next 2 rows, then 3 sts at beg of foll 2 rows, *BO 2 sts at beg of foll 2 rows, then 1 st at beg of foll 2 rows; rep from * 1 (1, 2, 2) more time(s), then BO 2 sts at beg of foll 2 rows, then 1 st at beg of foll 14 (18, 18, 22) rows, then 3 sts at beg of next 4 rows—17 (17, 19, 19) sts rem. BO all sts.

Finishing

Block to measurements. Place 15 (15, 19, 20) held right-front and right-back shoulder sts onto needles. With RS tog and using the three-needle BO (see Glossary), join shoulder sts. Rep for left shoulder. Sew side seams.

Neckband

With size 2 needles and RS facing, beg at left edge of placket with chart Row 1 (5, 9, 13), work 24 (24, 25, 25) held left-back sts in patt as established, pick up and knit 3 (3, 1, 1) st(s) at shoulder, work 45 (45, 47, 47) held front sts in patt as established, pick up and knit 3 (3, 1, 1) st(s) at shoulder, work 24 (24, 25, 25) held right-back sts in patt as established—99 sts. *Note:* Patt should flow continuously around neckband.

Keeping first and last st in garter st for selvedge sts, work even in patt for 27 (23, 27, 27) more rows, ending with chart Row 28 (28, 8, 12)—band measures 3 (2½, 3, 3)" (7.5 (6.5, 7.5, 7.5] cm). BO all sts.

Placket Border

With crochet hook and RS facing, beg at right edge of placket, work 35 single crochet (sc; see Glossary for crochet instructions) to bottom of placket opening, 1 sc at base of placket, and 35 sc up left side of placket—71 sc total. Work 1 row even in sc. Work 1 row of picot crochet as foll: Sl st in first sc, *ch 3, skip 1 sc, sl st in each of next 4 sc*; rep from * to * 5 more times, ch 3, skip 1 sc, sl st in each of last 3 sc on right side of placket, sl st in center sc, sl st in each of first 3 sc on left side of placket; rep from * to * 6 times, ch 3, skip 1 sc, sl st in last sc.

Sew seven buttons onto left side of placket between the first 2 sc rows and opposite the 7 picots on the right side of placket. Sew sleeve seams. Set in sleeves. Weave in loose ends.

Wakame
LACE TUNIC

Angela Hahn
Interweave Knits, SUMMER 2008

This top grew naturally out of a Japanese stitch pattern of leaves and flowers. After the lower body is worked from side to side, the upper body and sleeves are worked in one piece to the shoulders. A luxurious silk-and-seaweed blend highlights the openwork and gives the fabric depth. Self-finished edges and narrow I-cord trim create clean, unfussy lines.

FINISHED SIZE

33$\frac{1}{4}$ (37, 40$\frac{3}{4}$, 44$\frac{1}{2}$, 49$\frac{1}{4}$, 53, 56$\frac{3}{4}$)" (84.5 [94, 103.5, 112.5, 125, 134.5, 144] cm) bust circumference. Tunic shown measures 37" (94 cm); modeled with about 5" (12.5 cm) positive ease.

YARN

DK weight (Light #3).

SHOWN HERE: Tilli Tomas Fil de la Mer (70% silk, 30% SeaCell; 140 yd [128 m]/50 g): #249 parchment, 8 (8, 9, 9, 11, 12, 12) skeins.

NEEDLES

Size 7 (4.5 mm): 24" to 40" (60 to 100 cm) circular (cir), depending on selected size, and one spare needle. Adjust needle size if necessary to obtain the correct gauge.

NOTIONS

Cable needle (cn); markers (m); waste yarn for provisional CO; stitch holders; tapestry needle.

GAUGE

21 sts and 28 rows = 4" (10 cm) in lace patt, after blocking.

STITCH GUIDE

Mini Eyelet Cable (MEC): (worked over 2 sts)

ROW 1: (RS) K2tog, yo.

ROWS 2 AND 4: Purl (if working in the rnd, knit).

ROW 3: Yo, ssk.

Rep Rows 1–4 for patt.

NOTES

To lengthen tunic by 4" (10 cm), CO 75 sts for lower body and repeat Lace chart three times instead of twice. Purchase 0 (1, 1, 1, 1, 1, 1) extra skein of yarn if lengthening tunic.

Tunic

Lower Body

Using the invisible provisional method (see Glossary), CO 54 sts.

NEXT ROW: (RS) Work Row 1 of Lace chart 2 times, [MEC (see Stitch Guide at left)] 5 times, p2.

NEXT ROW: (WS) K2, [MEC] 5 times, work Row 2 of Lace chart 2 times.

Cont as established, work Rows 1–12 of Lace chart a total of 18 (21, 23, 25, 28, 30, 32) times, then work Rows 1–11 of chart once more—piece measures about 32½ (37½, 41, 44½, 49½, 53, 56½)" (82.5 [95, 104, 113, 125.5, 134.5, 143.5] cm) from CO.

Lace

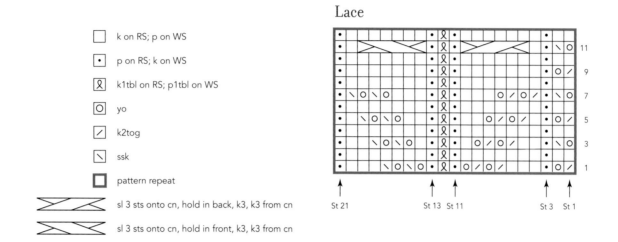

□	k on RS; p on WS
·	p on RS; k on WS
ℓ	k1tbl on RS; p1tbl on WS
O	yo
/	k2tog
\	ssk
▢	pattern repeat

sl 3 sts onto cn, hold in back, k3, k3 from cn

sl 3 sts onto cn, hold in front, k3, k3 from cn

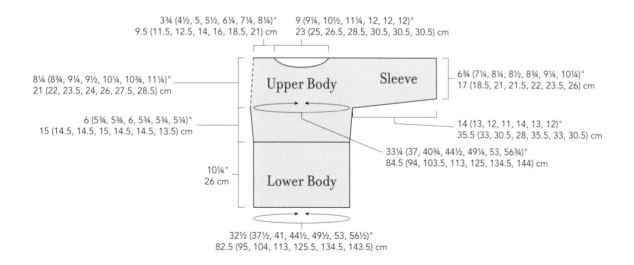

3¾ (4½, 5, 5½, 6¼, 7¼, 8¼)"
9.5 (11.5, 12.5, 14, 16, 18.5, 21) cm

9 (9¼, 10½, 11¼, 12, 12, 12)"
23 (25, 26.5, 28.5, 30.5, 30.5, 30.5) cm

8¼ (8¾, 9¼, 9½, 10¼, 10¾, 11¼)"
21 (22, 23.5, 24, 26, 27.5, 28.5) cm

Upper Body   Sleeve

6¾ (7¼, 8¼, 8½, 8¾, 9¼, 10¼)"
17 (18.5, 21, 21.5, 22, 23.5, 26) cm

6 (5¾, 5¾, 6, 5¾, 5¾, 5¼)"
15 (14.5, 14.5, 15, 14.5, 14.5, 13.5) cm

14 (13, 12, 11, 14, 13, 12)"
35.5 (33, 30.5, 28, 35.5, 33, 30.5) cm

33¼ (37, 40¾, 44½, 49¼, 53, 56¾)"
84.5 (94, 103.5, 113, 125, 134.5, 144) cm

10¼"
26 cm   Lower Body

32½ (37½, 41, 44½, 49½, 53, 56½)"
82.5 (95, 104, 113, 125.5, 134.5, 143.5) cm

Remove provisional CO and place sts on spare needle. With RS tog and using the three-needle BO (see Glossary), join short ends of piece, being careful not to twist.

Upper Body

With RS facing and beg at seam, pick up and knit 174 (194, 214, 234, 258, 278, 298) sts evenly spaced along purled edge (about 3 sts for every 4 rows). Place marker (pm) for right side and join in the rnd. Beg with Row 1 of Lace chart, set up patt as foll:

SIZE 33¼" (84.5 CM) ONLY

*Work Sts 11–21 of Lace chart, work Sts 1–21 of chart 3 times, work Sts 1–13 of chart; place marker (pm) for left side and rep from * to end of rnd.

SIZE 37" (94 CM) ONLY

*P1, k1tbl, p1, MEC, work Sts 11–21 of Lace chart, work Sts 1–21 of chart 3 times, work Sts 1–13 of chart, MEC, p1, k1tbl, p1; pm for left side and rep from * to end of rnd.

SIZE 40¾" (103.5) ONLY

*Work Lace chart 5 times, MEC; pm for left side and rep from * to end of rnd.

SIZE 44½" (113 CM) ONLY

*P1, k1tbl, p1, MEC, work Lace chart 5 ties, [MEC] 2 times, p1, k1tbl, p1; pm for left side and rep from * to end of rnd.

SIZE 49¼" (125 CM) ONLY

*Work Sts 11–21 of Lace chart, work Sts 1–21 of chart 5 times, work Sts 1–13 of chart; pm for left side and rep from * to end of rnd.

SIZE 53" (134.5) ONLY

*P1, k1tbl, p1, MEC, work Sts 11–21 of Lace chart, work Sts 1–21 of chart 5 times, work Sts 1–13 of chart, MEC, p1, k1tbl, p1; pm for left side and rep from * to end of rnd.

SIZE 56¾" (144 CM) ONLY

*Work Lace chart 7 times, MEC; pm for left side and rep from * to end of rnd.

ALL SIZES

Cont as established until a total of 42 (36, 40, 38, 40, 36, 36) rnds have been worked.

SIZES 37 (44½, 53)" (94 [113, 134.5] CM) ONLY

NEXT RND: *Work to 3 sts before next m, [MEC] 3 times (remove/replace m after 2nd k2tog or before 2nd ssk); rep from * once more—3 sts past end-of-rnd m. Complete this rnd in patt, then work in patt for 2 more rnds.

Divide for Front and Back

SIZES 37 (53)" (94 [134.5] CM) ONLY

NEXT RND: K5, work to 5 sts before next m, k2, yo, ssk, yo, k1, CO 15 sts for left sleeve using the backward-loop method (see page 55).

SIZE 44½" (113 CM) ONLY:

NEXT RND: K4, p1, work to 5 sts before next m, p1, [k2tog, yo] 2 times, CO 16 sts for left sleeve using the backward-loop method.

SIZES 33¼ (40¾, 49¼, 56¾)" (84.5 [103.5, 125, 144] CM) ONLY

Work to next m, CO 16 sts for left sleeve using the backward-loop method.

ALL SIZES

Place 87 (97, 107, 117, 129, 139, 149) unworked sts between left-side and right-side markers on holder for front and cont to work back/sleeves only—103 (113, 123, 133, 145, 155, 165) sts rem.

SIZES 37 (44½, 53)" ONLY

NEXT ROW: (WS) P16 sleeve sts, p5 (4, 5), k0 (1, 0), cont in patt to last 5 sts, p5 (0, 5), k0 (1, 0), p0 (4, 0).

P16 sleeve sts, cont in patt to end of row.

ALL SIZES

At end of row just completed, CO 16 sts for right sleeve—119 (129, 139, 149, 161, 171, 181) sts.

NEXT ROW: (RS) Keeping patt continuous across back, work lace patt across all sts to end of row, then CO 16 sts for left sleeve—135 (145, 155, 165, 177, 187, 197) sts.

NEXT ROW: (WS) P16 sleeve sts, work in patt to end of row, CO 16 sts for right sleeve—151 (161, 171, 181, 193, 203, 213) sts.

Rep last 2 rows 2 (2, 1, 1, 2, 2, 1) time(s)—215 (225, 203, 213, 257, 267, 245) sts.

Work 2 more rows as established, CO 9 (4, 15, 10, 9, 4, 15) sts at end of each row for sleeves—233 (233, 233, 233, 275, 275, 275) sts. Work even for a total of 99 (101, 105, 109, 111, 115, 115) upper-body rows, ending with a RS row—piece measures about 14¼ (14½, 15, 15½, 15¾, 16½, 16½)" (36 [37, 38, 39.5, 40, 42, 42] cm) from pick-up. Break yarn, leaving a long tail. Place sts on holder.

Front

Join yarn with RS facing. Work as for back through sleeve shaping, ending with Row 88 (90, 94, 98, 100, 104, 104) of upper body—233 (233, 233, 233, 275, 275, 275) sts.

SHAPE NECK

On Row 89 (91, 95, 99, 101, 105, 105), work 108 (108, 108, 108, 129, 129, 129) sts in patt, ending with St 3 of center-front Lace rep. Place next 125 (125, 125, 125, 146, 146, 146) sts on holder. BO 5 (6, 7, 8, 9, 9, 9) sts at beg of next 2 WS rows—98 (96, 94, 92, 111, 111, 111) sts rem.

Dec 1 st in patt at neck edge every row 5 times (ssk on RS, ssp [see Glossary] on WS)—93 (91, 89, 87, 106, 106, 106) sts

rem. Work 2 rows even, ending with a RS row. Break yarn. Place sts on holder.

With RS facing, join yarn to right-front/sleeve sts at center front. BO 17 sts, work to end of row—108 (108, 108, 108, 129, 129, 129) sts rem.

BO 5 (6, 7, 8, 9, 9, 9) sts at beg of next 2 RS rows—98 (96, 94, 92, 111, 111, 111) sts rem.

Dec 1 st at neck edge every row 5 times (p2tog on WS, k2tog on RS)—93 (91, 89, 87, 106, 106, 106) sts rem. Work 1 RS row even. Do not break yarn.

Finishing

Turn tunic inside out. Using working yarn and the three-needle method, join right sleeve and shoulder from cuff to neck edge. Do not break yarn. Using long yarn tail and the three-needle method, join left sleeve and shoulder from cuff to neck edge. Place rem 47 (51, 55, 59, 63, 63, 63) back neck sts on needle. Turn tunic right side out.

Neckband

With WS facing and beg at right shoulder seam, use working yarn to pick up and purl 5 sts along angled right-front neck, 37 (41, 45, 49, 53, 53, 53) sts along BO edge, and 5 sts along angled left-front neck—94 (102, 110, 118, 126, 126, 126) sts total. Turn work to RS and, using the knitted method (see page 55), CO 2 sts—96 (104, 112, 120, 128, 128, 128) sts. BO as foll: *K1, ssk, place 2 sts on right needle onto left needle; rep from * until all front and back neck sts have been worked—2 sts rem on left needle. Break yarn. With yarn threaded on a tapestry needle, use the Kitchener method (see Glossary) to graft these 2 sts to beg of neckband. Sew underarm seams, adjusting yarn tension in underarm areas if necessary to even out mesh created by multiple yo's and dec's.

Weave in loose ends. Block to measurements.

Dorflinger TEE

FINISHED SIZE

31 (34½, 38, 43½, 47, 50½, 54)"
(79 [87.5, 96.5, 128.5, 137] cm) bust
circumference; sweater shown
measures 34½" (87.5 cm).

YARN

Bulky (Bulky #5).

SHOWN HERE: Elann.com
Peruvian Highland Chunky (100%
wool; 76 yd [70 m]/50 g): #0620
garnet, 4 (4, 5, 5, 6, 7, 7) skeins.

NEEDLES

Size 10¾ (7 mm): 16" (40 cm) and
24" (60 cm) circular (cir) and set of
double-pointed (dpn). Adjust needle
size if necessary to obtain the correct
gauge.

NOTIONS

Size K/10½ (6.5 mm) crochet hook;
waste yarn; markers (m); tapestry
needle; row counter (optional);
blocking wires (optional); rust-proof
pins

GAUGE

10 sts and 17 rows = 4" (10 cm) in St st
and in 1×1 garter rib, after blocking;
10 sts of lace patt = 4½" (11.5 cm)
wide, after blocking; 20 rows of lace
patt = 4¾" (12 cm) tall, after blocking.

Mandy Moore

Knitscene, FALL 2010

Chunky yarn and lace are an uncommon pairing, but
they combine in the Dorflinger Tee to create bold,
graphic motifs on a large scale. The diamond shapes in
the blocked-out negative space create a sheer layering
piece. The top-down tee is worked in the round, with
sleeves that grow from increases along raglan lines.

STITCH GUIDE

1×1 Garter Rib: (even number of sts)

RND 1: Knit.

RND 2: *P1, k1; rep from * around.

Rep Rnds 1 and 2 for patt.

···

Raglan-Seam Stitches (r-seam sts):
(worked over 1 [1, 1, 3, 3, 3, 3] st[s])
For first 3 sizes, there is a single st between
each pair of m for raglan seam; knit these
sts on odd-numbered rnds and purl them on
even-numbered rnds. For rem sizes there are
3 sts for raglan seam between each pair of m;
knit these 3 sts on odd-numbered rnds, work
[p1, k1, p1] over each set of 3 sts on even-
numbered rnds.

NOTES

Tee is worked from the neck down in an
allover lace pattern (see charts), which is
offset by 5 stitches every 10 rounds. Lace
continues from the neck edge (yoke and
sleeves) to beginning of garter rib at lower
edge. Raglan seams and underarm seams
are worked in 1×1 garter rib throughout, with
the lace pattern centered between the seam
stitches.

Tee
Yoke

NECK EDGING

With shorter cir needle and the crochet-chain provisional
method (see Glossary), CO 36 (36, 36, 44, 44, 44, 44) sts.
Place marker (pm) and join for working in the rnd, being
careful not to twist sts. Knit 3 rnds.

Fold work to RS so that CO edge is directly in front of
working needle, with WS facing. Carefully remove waste yarn
from a few CO sts at a time and place live sts on a dpn.

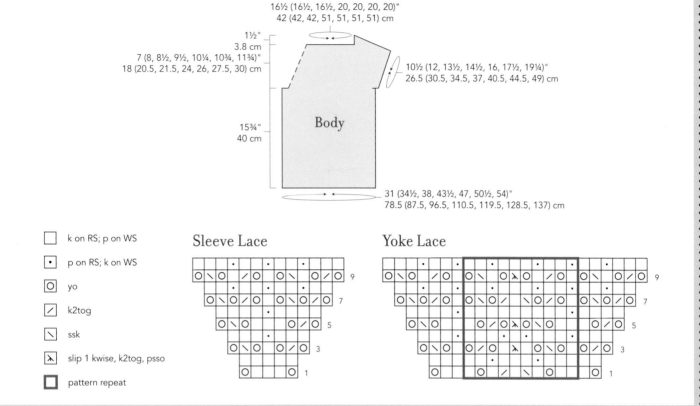

16½ (16½, 16½, 20, 20, 20, 20)"
42 (42, 42, 51, 51, 51, 51) cm

1½"
3.8 cm

7 (8, 8½, 9½, 10¼, 10¾, 11¾)"
18 (20.5, 21.5, 24, 26, 27.5, 30) cm

10½ (12, 13½, 14½, 16, 17½, 19¼)"
26.5 (30.5, 34.5, 37, 40.5, 44.5, 49) cm

15¾"
40 cm

Body

31 (34½, 38, 43½, 47, 50½, 54)"
78.5 (87.5, 96.5, 110.5, 119.5, 128.5, 137) cm

☐ k on RS; p on WS

• p on RS; k on WS

O yo

∕ k2tog

∖ ssk

⅄ slip 1 kwise, k2tog, psso

☐ pattern repeat

Sleeve Lace

Yoke Lace

Join edging with working needle as foll: *p2tog (CO st with st from working needle); rep from * until all sts are joined.

RAGLAN

SET-UP RND: K1 (1, 1, 3, 3, 3, 3) for r-seam (see Stitch Guide at left), pm, k3 for sleeve, pm, k1 (1, 1, 3, 3, 3, 3) for r-seam, pm, k13 for front (one 10-st lace rep + 3 edge sts), pm, k1 (1, 1, 3, 3, 3, 3) for r-seam, pm, k3 for sleeve, pm, k1 (1, 1, 3, 3, 3, 3) for r-seam, pm, k13 for back (one 10-st lace rep + 3 edge sts).

Work 1 rnd even, knitting sts for front, back, and sleeves and working r-seams in patt (see Stitch Guide).

RND 1: Cont r-seams as established, work Yoke Lace and Sleeve Lace charts on front, back, and sleeve sts as foll: *work r-seam over 1 (1, 1, 3, 3, 3, 3) st(s), sl m, work Rnd 1 of Sleeve Lace chart, sl m, work r-seam, sl m, work Rnd 1 of Yoke Lace chart; rep from * once—44 (44, 44, 52, 52, 52, 52) sts.

Maintaining r-seams, work Rnds 2–10 from charts, working inc'd sts in patt—76 (76, 76, 84, 84, 84, 84) sts: 23 sts each for front and back (two 10-st lace reps + 3 edge sts), 13 sts for each sleeve (one 10-st lace rep + 3 edge sts), plus 4 (4, 4, 12, 12, 12, 12) sts for r-seams.

Changing to longer cir needle when necessary, working sleeves from Yoke Lace chart instead of Sleeve Lace chart, work 8 (12, 14, 18, 22, 24, 28) rnds in patt as foll: Cont incs as established, rep Rnds 1–10 (*Note:* Size 31" (79 cm) only ends on Rnd 8 of first rep) on all sections, working additional 10-st lace reps every 10 rnds as sts become available, ending with Rnd 8 (2, 4, 8, 2, 4, 8) of Yoke and Sleeve Lace charts—108 (124, 132, 156, 172, 180, 196) sts.

NEXT RND: *Work r-seam, sl m, work Rnd 1 of Body Lace chart for your size to next m, sl m; rep from * 3 times. Work 2 rnds even in patt.

DIVIDE FOR SLEEVES

DIVIDING RND: (Rnd 4 of Body Lace chart) Work in patt to 2nd m, place last 21 (25, 27, 31, 35, 37, 41) sts worked (all sts between first and 2nd m) on waste yarn for first sleeve, removing first and 2nd m; work in patt to 6th m, place last 21 (25, 27, 31, 35, 37, 41) sts worked (all sts between 5th and 6th m) on waste yarn for 2nd sleeve, removing 5th and 6th m; work in patt to end.

NEXT RND: (Rnd 5 of Body Lace chart) *K1 (1, 1, 3, 3, 3, 3), CO 1 (1, 3, 1, 1, 3, 3) st(s) using the backward-loop method, k1 (1, 1, 3, 3, 3, 3) for underarm*, sl m, work in patt to next m, sl m, rep from * to * for underarm, sl m, work in patt to end—68 (76, 84, 96, 104, 112, 120) sts for body: 31 (35, 37, 41, 45, 47, 51) sts each for front and back, 3 (3, 5, 7, 7, 9, 9) sts between m at each underarm.

Lower Body

SET-UP RND: *[P1, k1] 1 (1, 2, 3, 3, 4, 4) time(s), p1, work next rnd of Body Lace chart over 31 (35, 37, 41, 45, 47, 51) sts; rep from * once. Underarm sts are worked in 1×1 garter rib (see Stitch Guide); front and back sts are worked foll Body Lace chart.

Work Rnds 7–20 once, Rnds 1–20 twice, then Rnds 21 and 22 once (Rnd 22 establishes 1×1 garter rib). Work 11 rnds in 1×1 garter rib over all sts. BO all sts using the sewn method.

Finishing
Armhole Edging

With RS facing and dpn, pick up and knit 5 (5, 7, 5, 5, 7, 7) sts along CO edge at underarm, k21 (25, 27, 31, 35, 37, 41) held sleeve sts, pm, and join in the rnd—26 (30, 34, 36, 40, 44, 48) sts. Knit 2 rnds. BO all sts with the sewn method.

Weave in ends. Block garment firmly to measurements shown on schematic.

Legend

- ☐ k on RS; p on WS
- • p on RS; k on WS
- ☐ yo (○)
- ☐ k2tog (╱)
- ☐ ssk (╲)
- ☐ slip 1 kwise, k2tog, psso (⋋)
- ☐ pattern repeat

Body Lace
(sizes 31", 43½", 54" [79, 110.5, 137 cm])

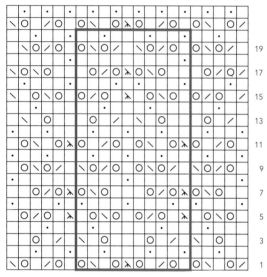

10 st repeat

Body Lace
(sizes 34½" and 47" [89.5 and 119.5 cm])

10 st repeat

Body Lace
(sizes 38" and 50½" [96.5 and 128.5 cm])

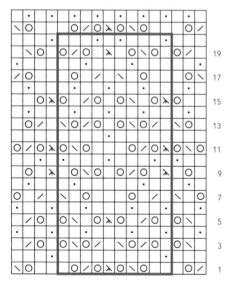

10 st repeat

Bleeding Hearts
STOLE

Anne Hanson
Interweave Knits, SPRING 2008

Anne Hanson was inspired by the first tiny shoots of bleeding hearts emerging in her garden. She says, "The tenderness of this coincidence informed the design—I intentionally kept the motifs small in scale to achieve a delicate look." Worked in two halves and grafted at the center back, the stole showcases bleeding hearts flanked by a winding pattern of airy leaves, daintily finished with a tiny loop-stitch edging.

FINISHED SIZE

23" (58.5 cm) wide and 84" (213.5 cm) long, blocked; 18" (45.5 cm) wide and 64" (162.5 cm) long, unblocked (gain in size is about 25%).

YARN

Laceweight (Lace #0).

SHOWN HERE: Jade Sapphire Silk/ Cashmere (55% silk, 45% cashmere; 400 yd [366 m]/55 g): #016 everglades, 3 balls.

NEEDLES

U.S. sizes 3 (3.25 mm) and 4 (3.5 mm): straight or 24" (60 cm) circular (cir). Adjust needle size if necessary to obtain the correct gauge.

NOTIONS

Markers (m); stitch holder; tapestry needle.

GAUGE

27 sts and 26 rows = 4" (10 cm) in main body panel patt on larger needle, after blocking.

NOTES

Throughout the stole, the stitch count will vary in the edgings and hem border patterns. Stitch count increases on Rows 1 and 11 of the hem border pattern and returns to the original number on Rows 9 and 19. The bleeding hearts motif increases on Rows 5 and 15 and returns to its original number on Rows 6 and 16.

Stole

First Half

HEM BORDER

With smaller needles and the knitted method (see page 55), loosely CO 105 sts as foll: CO 7 sts, place marker (pm), CO 91 sts, pm, CO 7 sts.

SET-UP ROW: (WS) K5, yo, k2tog, sl m, p91, sl m, k7.

Note: On first rep of Hem Border chart, do not work first 3 BO sts on Row 1 (i.e., beg Row 1 with k5).

Work Rows 1–20 of Hem Border chart 2 times, then work Rows 1–5 once more.

Work Row 6 of chart as foll to set up for next section: Work left edging, sl m, p13, pm, p95, pm, p13, sl m, work right edging—141 sts total; 10 left-edging sts, 13 left-border sts, 95 main-panel sts, 13 right-border sts, 10 right-edging sts. This completes the hem border section; the markers are now in place to work the transition section. The new markers mark the division between the leaf border that runs up each side of the stole's main panel and the bleeding hearts section that makes up the center of the stole.

TRANSITION SECTION

Change to larger needles and work Rows 1–10 of Transition chart—piece measures about 7" (18 cm) from CO; 138 sts total: 7 left-edging sts, 13 left-border sts, 95 main-panel sts, 13 right-border sts, 10 right-edging sts.

MAIN-BODY SECTION

Work Rows 1–20 of Main-Body Panel chart 10 times—piece measures about 32" (81.5) from CO. Cut yarn, leaving a 72" (183 cm) tail. Place all sts on a holder while second half of stole is worked.

Second Half

Work as for first half but end the last chart rep of Main-Body Panel with Row 14.

Work Row 15 as foll: BO 3 sts, knit to 2 sts before m, yo, k2tog, sl m, ssk, yo, k5, [yo, k1] 3 times, sl m, k2tog, k3, yo, k1, *yo, k4, sl 1, k2tog, psso, k4, yo, k1; rep from * to 5 sts before m, yo, k3, ssk, sl m, [k1, yo] 3 times, k5, yo, k2tog, sl m, k2, yo, k2tog, k6. Break yarn, leaving a 40" (101.5 cm) tail.

Finishing

Place each stole half on a separate needle. Holding needles parallel with WS tog, graft the sts tog using Kitchener st (see Glossary), working partway across using shorter tail, then working remainder using longer tail. Soak stole in lukewarm water with wool soap for about an hour or until fiber is fully saturated. Roll in a towel and squeeze out excess moisture. Stretch and pin piece to the finished dimensions. Allow to dry completely; piece may be steamed and air-dried as a final step to encourage fiber to bloom.

Chart Legend

□	k on RS; p on WS
•	p on RS; k on WS
O	yo
∕	k2tog on RS; p2tog on WS
\	ssk on RS; ssp on WS (see Glossary)
⟍	p2tog on RS; k2tog on WS
⋏	k3tog on RS; p3tog on WS
⋋	sl 1, k2tog, psso
⋏₃	k3tog through back loop (tbl) on RS; p3tog tbl on WS
⋏	sl 2 as if to k2tog, k1, p2sso
(shaded)	no stitch
⌒	BO 1 st
▭	pattern repeat
❘	marker position

Hem Border

left edging   main panel   right border   right edging

Transition

Main-Body Panel

FINISHED SIZE

39 (42, 45, 48, 52)" (99 [106.5, 114.5, 122, 132] cm) bust circumference; to fit bust size 32 (35, 38, 41, 44)" (81.5 [89, 96.5, 104, 112] cm); 5¾ (6½, 7½, 8¼, 9)" (14.5 [16.5, 19, 21, 23] cm) upper sleeve width. Sweater shown measures 42" (106.5 cm).

YARN

Worsted weight (Medium #4) and sewing thread.

SHOWN HERE: Jaeger Persia (82% Merino, 18% polyamid; 109 yd [100 m]/50 g): #505 flannel or #503 burgundy, 7 (8, 9, 10, 10) balls. *Note: This yarn has been discontinued; try substituting Rowan Lima.* Small spool of matching all-purpose sewing thread.

NEEDLES

Size 7 (4.5 mm): 32" (80 cm) circular (cir). Adjust needle size if necessary to obtain the correct gauge.

NOTIONS

Size G/6 (4.25 mm) crochet hook; markers (m); stitch holders; tapestry needle; four ¾" (2 cm) buttons.

GAUGE

16 sts and 24 rows = 4" (10 cm) in St st with yarn.

Scribble
LACE

Debbie New
Interweave Knits, SUMMER 2001

Debbie New pioneered the idea of using different yarn weights to achieve a lacy look with a simple stitch, which she dubbed "scribble lace." When confined within the yoke, the lace is so flexible that it adapts to the shape and weight of the rest of the knitting. This striking sweater has vertical lines and fitted sleeves for easy and elegant wearing.

STITCH GUIDE

Panel A:

(Basic 11-row panel worked with 2 balls of yarn at hem edge; alternate between the 2 balls every 2 rows.)

ROW 1: (RS) Knit to yoke m, k21 (20, 19, 18, 17), drop yarn and pick up thread, wrap thread around last st knitted, then k10 (lace section) with thread, wrap thread around next yarn st, turn.

ROWS 2 AND 10: With thread p10, with yarn purl to last 6 sts, sl 1, p5.

ROW 3: Knit to 2 sts past yoke m, turn.

ROWS 4, 6, AND 8: Sl 1 kwise, purl to last 6 sts, sl 1, p5.

ROW 5: Knit to last st before gap formed by turn, pick up a st by passing left needle down through st below, then k2tog, knit to last 15 sts (lace section), wrap thread around last st knitted, turn.

ROW 7: Knit to 10 sts past yoke m, turn.

ROW 9: Rep Row 1, closing gap at turn as in Row 5.

ROW 11: (garter ridge) With RS facing, k6, purl to last 5 sts, k5. Yarn is now at neck edge.

....

Panel B:

(Basic 11-row panel worked with one ball of yarn at hem edge.)

ROW 1: (RS) Knit to yoke m, k21 (20, 19, 18, 17), drop yarn and pick up thread, wrap thread around last st knitted, knit 10 (lace section) with thread, wrap thread

around next yarn st, sl rem 5 sts to right needle, turn, with yarn k5, turn, with yarn k5, sl these 5 sts back onto left needle, turn.

ROWS 2 AND 10: With thread p10, with yarn purl to last 6 sts, sl 1, p5.

ROW 3: Knit to 2 sts past yoke m, turn.

ROWS 4, 6, AND 8: Sl 1 kwise, purl to last 6 sts, sl 1, p5.

ROW 5: Knit to last st before gap formed by turn, pick up a st by passing left needle down through st below, then k2tog, knit to last 15 sts (lace section), wrap thread around last st knitted, turn.

ROW 7: Knit to 10 sts past yoke m, turn.

ROW 9: (RS) Knit to yoke m, k21 (20, 19, 18, 17) closing gap at previous turn, drop yarn and pick up thread, wrap thread around last st knitted, k10 (lace section) with thread, wrap thread around next yarn st, turn.

ROW 11: (garter ridge) With WS facing, knit to last 6 sts, p6. Yarn is now at hem edge.

....

Shaping Panel:

ROWS 1, 2, 3, 7, AND 9: (RS) Beg at hem edge, knit to yoke m, turn.

ROWS 2, 4, 6, AND 8: Sl 1 kwise, purl to last 6 sts, sl 1, p5.

ROW 10: (garter ridge) Knit to last 6 sts, p6.

NOTES

The sweater begins with the buttonhole loop at the back neck. Then stitches are cast on for the total length, and the entire garment is worked sideways in a single piece from center back to center back. Live sts are grafted onto the cast-on sts to join the two halves of the back.

....

The stitches used in this sweater are simple, and the pattern repeats in panels. The challenge lies in handling the thread and yarn together and in keeping track of the short-rows used for shaping the yoke.

....

The body and sleeves are fitted. In choosing a size, consider upper sleeve width as well as underarm circumference.

....

Much of the shaping is worked with short-rows as foll: Work to the turn point, turn, slip the first stitch after turning, work to end. On the following row, knit the last stitch before the gap, pick up a stitch by passing the left needle down through the stitch below the one just knitted, then k2tog.

....

Take particular care when knitting with the thin thread on such large needles to ensure that only 1 stitch is worked at a time.

....

To prevent holes at the boundaries between the yarn and thread sections, wrap the thread around the adjacent yarn stitch at the beg and end of the thread sections on every RS thread row.

....

The body panels usually repeat over an odd number of rows; the first panel ends with the yarn at the neck edge, then a new ball of yarn is joined at the hem edge to work the second panel. The final row of most panels alternates between being a right-side row and a wrong-side row.

Pullover
Right Back

Pull out 3 yd (3 m) of yarn from ball, make a slipknot, and place on crochet hook. Using the tail end of the yarn, work a crochet chain (ch; see Glossary) 60 sts long. Remove crochet hook. With cir needle, and using the ball end of yarn, pick up and knit 1 st into the first st of the chain (opposite the end with the loop), *skip 5 ch-sp, pick up and knit 1 st in 6th ch-sp, pass second st on needle over first (to form buttonhole loop), pick up and knit 1 st in each of the next 4 ch-sp; rep from * 3 more times—4 button loops; 17 sts. Ravel remaining loops of chain and use both the tail and ball ends of yarn in the long-tail method (see Glossary) to CO 19 (18, 17, 16, 15) sts for yoke, place marker (pm) for yoke, and CO 62 (64, 66, 68, 70) sts for body—98 (99, 100, 101, 102) sts total.

Panel 1

Work Panel A (see Stitch Guide at left); yarn is at neck edge. Do not cut yarn.

Panel 2

Join new yarn at hem edge and with RS facing, work Panel B (see Stitch Guide) with the foll changes:

ROW 3: Inc 1 st in yoke as foll: Knit to yoke m, work lifted inc (see Glossary), sl m, k2, turn—1 st inc'd.

ROW 7: Inc 1 st in yoke as foll: Knit to yoke m, lifted inc, sl m, k10, turn—1 st inc'd.

For sizes 48" and 52" (122 and 132 cm) only: work an extra garter ridge at neck edge by substituting Row 1 for Row 9.

After Row 11—5 neckband sts, 10 sts in lace section, 21 (20, 19, 18, 17) yoke sts, 58 (60, 62, 64, 66) body sts, 6 hem sts.

Panel 3

Work Panel A and *at the same time* work a lifted inc before yoke m on Rows 3, 5, and 7 (3 sts inc'd). After Row 11—5 neckband sts, 10 lace sts, 21 (20, 19, 18, 17) yoke sts, 61 (63, 65, 67, 69) body sts, 6 hem sts.

Panel 4

Work Panel B and *at the same time* work a lifted inc before yoke m on Rows 3, 5, and 7 (3 sts inc'd).

For size 52" (132 cm) only: Work an extra garter ridge at neck edge by substituting Row 1 for Row 9. After Row 11—5 neckband sts, 10 lace sts, 21 (20, 19, 18, 17) yoke sts, 64 (66, 68, 70, 72) body sts, 6 hem sts.

Panel 5

Work Panel A and *at the same time* work a lifted inc before yoke m on Rows 3, 5, 7, and 9 (4 sts inc'd).

After Row 11—5 neckband sts, 10 lace sts, 21 (20, 19, 18, 17) yoke sts, 68 (70, 72, 74, 76) body sts, 6 hem sts. There should be 5 (5, 5, 6, 7) garter ridges at neck edge, including the first ridge at base of button loops.

SHAPE RIGHT ARMHOLE

Work Shaping Panel for 5 (5, 9, 15, 19) rows and *at the same time* dec 1 st at armhole edge every row as foll:

ROWS 1, 3, 5, 7, AND 9: Knit to 2 sts before yoke m, k2tog, turn.

ROWS 2, 4, 6, AND 8: P2tog, purl to last 6 sts, sl 1, p5.

ROW 10: (garter ridge) K2tog, knit to last 6 sts, p6.

Cont to work 4 (10, 10, 10, 10) more rows without dec, ending with Row 9 (5, 9, 5, 9)—5 (5, 9, 15, 19) body sts dec'd: 5 neckband sts, 10 lace sts, 21 (20, 19, 18, 17) yoke sts, 63 (65, 63, 59, 57) body sts, 6 hem sts.

Place body and hem sts on holder. Keeping neckband and yoke sts on needle and yoke m in place, with RS facing, yarn at armhole edge, and using the backward-loop method (see page 55), CO 12 (9, 8, 4, 6) sts for sleeve. There will be a gap between the yoke and sleeve sts on the needle; yarn is ready to work a RS row.

Right Sleeve

SHAPE SLEEVE BACK AND JOIN TO BODY

Work Shaping Panel to work sleeve sts only and *at the same time* omit hem on WS rows.

Beg with Row 1 (7, 1, 7, 1), work 6 (10, 10, 10, 10) rows with the foll changes to RS and WS rows: RS rows: Work to last sleeve st, sl 1, pick up and knit 1 st from selvedge edge of right back armhole, psso. WS rows: Work to end of row, CO 14 (10, 8, 7, 6) sts. Align garter ridges of sleeve with garter ridges of back as you pick up. End having just worked Row 6 (6, 10, 6, 10)—54 (59, 48, 39, 36) sleeve sts.

Beg with Row 7 (7, 1, 7, 1), work 4 (4, 8, 10, 12) more rows as foll: RS rows: Work to end of row, pick up and knit 2 sts from selvedge edge of right back armhole. WS rows: Work to end of row, CO 14 (10, 7, 7, 6) sts. Replace hem m 6 sts from hem edge.

Work 0 (0, 2, 4, 8) more rows of Shaping Panel without casting on any more sleeve sts, but cont to pick up 2 sts on RS rows. End having just worked Row 10—80 (77, 80, 82, 86) sleeve sts, 6 hem sts. Make sure yoke m is still in place.

Panel 1

Work Panel B and *at the same time* dec 1 st before yoke m (k2tog) on Rows 3 and 7 (2 sts dec'd).

For size 52" (132 cm) only: work an extra garter ridge at neck edge by substituting Row 1 for Row 9. After Row 11—5 neckband sts, 10 lace sts, 21 (20, 19, 18, 17) yoke sts, 78 (75, 78, 80, 84) sleeve sts, 6 hem sts.

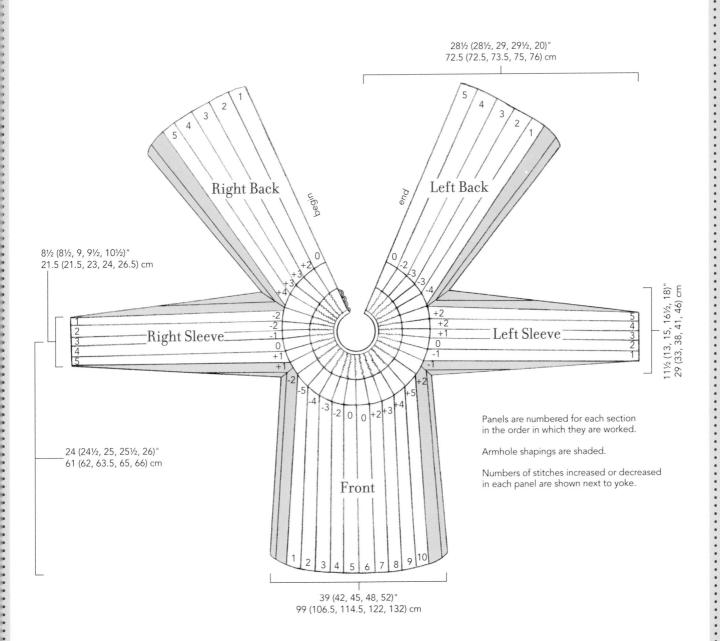

28½ (28½, 29, 29½, 20)"
72.5 (72.5, 73.5, 75, 76) cm

Right Back

begin

end

Left Back

8½ (8½, 9, 9½, 10½)"
21.5 (21.5, 23, 24, 26.5) cm

+2
+3
+4
0

0
-2
-3
-4

Right Sleeve

-2
-2
-1
0
+1
+1

1
2
3
4
5

Left Sleeve

+2
+2
+1
0
-1

5
4
3
2
1

11½ (13, 15, 16½, 18)"
29 (33, 38, 41, 46) cm

-2
-5
-4
-3
-2
0
0
+2
+3
+4
+5

+2
+5

24 (24½, 25, 25½, 26)"
61 (62, 63.5, 65, 66) cm

Front

Panels are numbered for each section
in the order in which they are worked.

Armhole shapings are shaded.

Numbers of stitches increased or decreased
in each panel are shown next to yoke.

1 2 3 4 5 6 7 8 9 10

39 (42, 45, 48, 52)"
99 (106.5, 114.5, 122, 132) cm

Panel 2

Alternate between the 2 balls of yarn every 2 rows. Work Panel A and *at the same time* dec 1 st before yoke m on Row 3 and 7 (2 sts dec'd).

Panel 3

Work Panel B and *at the same time,* for size 39" (99 cm) only, omit a garter ridge at neck by substituting Row 9 for Row 1; k2tog before yoke m on Row 5; and for sizes 45" and 48" (114.5 and 122 cm) only, add a garter ridge at neck edge by substituting Row 1 for Row 9. After Row 11, 1 st dec'd.

Panel 4

Work Panel A.

Panel 5

Work Panel B and *at the same time* work a lifted-inc before yoke m on Row 5; for size 52 only, add a garter ridge at neck edge by substituting Row 1 for Row 9. After Row 11, 1 st inc'd—5 neckband sts, 10 lace sts, 21 (20, 19, 18, 17) yoke sts, 76 (73, 76, 78, 82) sleeve sts, 6 hem sts.

SHAPE SLEEVE FRONT

Remove hem m. Work Rows 1–4 of Panel A and *at the same time* BO 14 (10, 7, 0, 0) sts at beg of Rows 1 and 3; work a lifted-inc before yoke m on Row 3. After Row 4, 1 st inc'd, 28 (20, 14, 0, 0) sts bound off. Cut off one ball of yarn, leaving one working ball—5 neckband sts, 10 lace sts, 21 (20, 19, 18, 17) yoke sts, 55 (60, 69, 79, 83) sleeve sts, 0 (0, 0, 6, 6) hem sts. There should be 10 (11, 12, 13, 15) garter ridges at neck edge, including the first ridge at base of button loops.

Cont with Row 5 of Shaping Panel as foll: For size 52" (132 cm) only, work 4 rows as written. For all sizes, remove hem m and cont for 0 (0, 6, 10, 12) rows with the foll changes to RS and WS rows: RS rows: BO 0 (0, 7, 7, 7) sts at beg of row, k2tog before yoke m. WS rows: P2tog at beg of row (work as k2tog in garter ridge). Then work 6 (10, 10, 10, 10) more rows without dec and *at the same time* BO 14 (10, 7, 7, 6) sts at beg of RS rows. BO rem 13 (10, 7, 5, 5) sleeve sts.

Front

SHAPE RIGHT ARMHOLE AND JOIN SLEEVE

Using the needle tip at the neck edge and beg with sts at hem edge, place held hem and body sts on needle, replacing hem and yoke markers as you go. Complete Row 10 (6, 10, 6, 10) on hem and body sts only—5 neckband sts, 10 lace sts, 21 (20, 19, 18, 17) yoke sts, 63 (65, 63, 59, 57) body sts, 6 hem sts.

Beg with Row 1 (7, 1, 7, 1) of Shaping Panel, work 6 (10, 10, 10, 10) rows with the foll changes: RS rows: Work to last body st, sl 1, pick up and knit 1 st from selvedge edge of right sleeve armhole, psso.

Cont working 0 (0, 6, 10, 16) rows as foll: RS Rows: At end of row, pick up and knit 2 sts from selvedge edge of right back armhole. End with Row 6 and yarn at hem edge—63 (65, 69, 69, 73) body sts, 6 hem sts.

Beg with Row 7, Work Panel A, and *at the same time* k2tog before yoke m on Rows 7 and 9 (2 sts dec'd). Join new ball of yarn at hem edge.

Panel 1

Work Panel B and *at the same time* k2tog before yoke m on Rows 1, 3, 5, 7, and 9 (5 sts dec'd); for sizes 42", 45", 48", and 52" (106.5, 114.5, 122, 132 cm) only: work an extra garter ridge at neck by substituting Row 1 for Row 9.

Panel 2

Work Panel A and *at the same time* k2tog before yoke m on Rows 1, 3, 5, and 7 (4 sts dec'd).

Panel 3

Work Panel B and *at the same time* k2tog before yoke m on Rows 3, 5, and 7 (3 sts dec'd); for sizes 48" and 52" (122 and 132 cm) only, work an extra garter ridge at neck by substituting Row 1 for Row 9.

Panel 4

Work Panel A, and *at the same time* k2tog before yoke m on Rows 1 and 5 (2 sts dec'd): 5 neckband sts, 10 lace sts, 21 (20, 19, 18, 17) yoke sts, 47 (49, 53, 53, 57): body sts, 6 hem sts.

Panel 5

Work Panel B and *at the same time* for sizes 45" and 52" (114.5 and 132 cm) only, work an extra garter ridge at neck by substituting Row 1 for Row 9.

Panel 6

Work Panel A.

Panel 7

Work Panel B and *at the same time* work a lifted inc before yoke m on Rows 5 and 9 (2 sts inc'd); for sizes 48" and 52" (122 and 132 cm) only, substitute Row 1 for Row 9.

Panel 8

Work Panel A and *at the same time* work a lifted inc before yoke m on Rows 3, 5, and 7 (3 sts inc'd).

Panel 9

Work Panel B and *at the same time* work a lifted inc before yoke m on Rows 1, 3, 5, and 7 (4 sts inc'd); for sizes 42", 45", 48", and 52" (106.5, 114.5, 122, and 132 cm) only: substitute Row 1 for Row 9.

Panel 10

Work Panel A and *at the same time* work a lifted inc before yoke m on Rows 1, 3, 5, 7, and 9 (5 sts inc'd): 5 neckband sts, 10 lace sts, 21 (20, 19, 18, 17) yoke sts, 61 (63, 67, 67, 71) body sts, 6 hem sts.

SHAPE LEFT ARMHOLE

Work Rows 1–4 of Panel B and *at the same time* work a lifted inc before yoke m on Rows 1 and 3 (2 sts inc'd). After Row 4 there will be 63 (65, 69, 69, 73) body sts, 6 hem sts, and 21 (24, 25, 28, 30) garter ridges at neck edge.

Beg with Row 5 of Shaping Panel, work 0 (0, 6, 10, 16) rows with the foll changes to RS and WS rows: RS rows: K2tog before yoke m. WS rows: P2tog at beg of row (k2tog in garter ridge).

Work 5 (11, 9, 11, 9) more rows without dec, ending with Row 9 (5, 9, 5, 9) of panel—63 (65, 63, 59, 57) body sts, 6 hem sts. Place 69 (71, 69, 65, 63) body and hem sts on holder.

Left Sleeve

SHAPE SLEEVE FRONT AND JOIN TO BODY

Keeping neckband and yoke sts on needle and yoke m in place, with RS facing, use yarn at armhole edge and backward-loop method to CO 13 (10, 8, 5, 5) sts for sleeve. Omit hem on WS rows and work Shaping Panel on sleeve sts only. Beg with Row 1 (7, 1, 7, 1) work 6 (10, 10, 10, 10) rows with the foll changes to RS and WS rows: RS rows: Work to last sleeve st, sl 1, pick up and knit 1 st from selvedge edge of right back armhole, psso. WS rows: Work to end of row, use backward-loop method to CO 14 (10, 9, 7, 6) sts. End having just worked Row 6 (6, 10, 6, 10)—55 (60, 53, 40, 37) sleeve sts.

Beg with Row 0 (0, 1, 7, 1), work 0 (0, 6, 10, 12) more rows with the foll changes to RS and WS rows: RS rows: At end of row, pick up and knit 2 sts from selvedge edge of right back armhole. WS rows: At end of row CO 0 (0, 8, 7, 7) sts. For all sizes, replace hem m when sleeve COs have been completed. For size 52" (132 cm) only, work 4 more rows of shaping panel without casting on more sts.

Beg with Row 5, work Panel B and *at the same time* CO 14 (10, 0, 0, 0) sts at end of Rows 6 and 8; replace hem m and k2tog before yoke m on Row 9—82 (79, 82, 84, 88) sleeve sts.

Panel 1

Work Panel A and *at the same time* k2tog before yoke m on Row 5 (1 st dec'd).

Panel 2

Work Panel B and *at the same time*, for size 39" (99 cm) only, omit a garter ridge at neck edge by substituting Row 9 for Row 1; for sizes 45", 48", and 52" (114.5, 122, and 132 cm) only, work an extra garter ridge at neck edge by substituting Row 1 for Row 9.

Panel 3

Work Panel A and *at the same time* work a lifted inc before yoke m on Row 5 (1 st inc'd).

Panel 4

Work Panel B and *at the same time* work a lifted inc before yoke m on Rows 3 and 7 (2 sts inc'd); for size 52" (132 cm) only, substitute Row 1 for Row 9.

Panel 5

Work Panel A and *at the same time* work a lifted inc before yoke m on Rows 5 and 9 (2 sts inc'd). After Row 11, remove hem marker—86 (83, 86, 88, 92) sleeve sts, 25 (29, 31, 34, 37) garter ridges at neck.

SHAPE SLEEVE BACK

Work Shaping Panel for 0 (0, 2, 4, 8) rows as written. Then work 4 (4, 8, 10, 12) rows with the foll changes to RS and WS rows: RS rows: BO 14 (10, 8, 7, 7) sts at beg of row, and k2tog before yoke m. WS rows: Dec 1 st at beg of row.

Cont to work 6 (10, 10, 10, 10) more rows and *at the same time* BO 14 (10, 7, 7, 6) sts at beg of RS rows. Then BO rem 12 (9, 11, 8, 8) sts. Yarn will be at armhole edge.

Left Back

SHAPE ARMHOLE AND JOIN SLEEVE

Using the needle tip at the neck edge and beg at hem edge, place 69 (71, 69, 65, 63) held hem and body sts on needle, replacing hem and yoke markers as you go. Complete Row 10 (6, 10, 6, 10) of Shaping Panel across hem and body sts only.

Beg with Row 1 (7, 1, 7, 1) of Shaping Panel, work 4 (10, 10, 10, 10) rows, working RS rows as foll: Work to last body st, sl 1, pick up and knit 1 st from selvedge edge of right sleeve armhole, psso. Work 6 (4, 10, 14, 20) rows more and *at the same time* pick up and knit 2 sts from selvedge edge at end of RS rows. End with Row 10 of Shaping Panel. Replace hem m—68 (69, 73, 73, 77) body sts, 6 hem sts.

Panel 1
Work Panel B and *at the same time* k2tog before yoke m on Rows 1, 3, 5, and 7 (4 sts dec'd); for size 52" (132 cm) only: Substitute Row 1 for Row 9.

Panel 2
Work Panel A and *at the same time* k2tog before yoke m on Rows 1, 3, and 7 (3 sts dec'd).

Panel 3
Work Panel B and *at the same time* k2tog before yoke m on Rows 1, 3, and 7 (3 sts dec'd).

Panel 4
Work Panel A and *at the same time* k2tog before yoke m on Rows 3 and 7 (2 sts dec'd).

Panel 5
Work Panel B and *at the same time* for sizes 48" and 52" (122 and 132 cm) only, substitute Row 1 for Row 9. There will be 31 (35, 37, 41, 45) garter ridges at neck edge.

Finishing
Use yarn at neck edge to BO 15 sts (neckband and lace section)—84 (83, 86, 85, 88) yoke, body, and hem sts rem. With yarn threaded on a tapestry needle, graft live sts for yoke, body, and hem to CO edge as shown at right. Thread 4 strands of thread on tapestry needle and sew sleeve seams. Turn hems to WS along slipped sts and sew in place using 4 strands of thread. Weave in loose ends. Sew buttons opposite button loops. Hang garment for 24 hours to allow it to stretch to final length.

Graft Center Back
Hold live sts of left back parallel to cast-on edge of right back. Bring tapestry needle back and forth between live stitches and cast-on edge (Figures 1 and 2), mimicking a row of knitting.

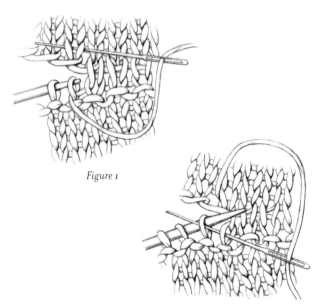

Figure 1

Figure 2

SCRIBBLE LACE

Bettie's Lace
STOCKINGS

Hana Jason
Interweave Knits, SPRING 2009

These socks use an easy but intricate-looking lace motif in long vertical stripes for vintage delicacy and sheerness—without using gossamer-light yarn. Working on only a handful of stitches, the pattern incorporates calf shaping into the lace motif, resulting in a stretchy, clingy stocking that stays up. A sweet picot bind-off and an eyelet round at the knee look modern on their own—or sweetly vintage with a ribbon garter.

FINISHED SIZE

7½" (19 cm) foot circumference; 8¾" (22 cm) from back of heel to tip of toe. One size fits most (see Notes on page 144). Sample socks modeled on a woman's U.S. size 8½ foot.

YARN

Fingering weight (Super Fine #1).

SHOWN HERE: Rowan 4 Ply Soft (100% merino; 191 yd [175 m]/50 g): #389 expresso (dark brown), 2 balls. *Note: This yarn has been discontinued; try Rowan Cashsoft 4 ply or Rowan Pure Wool 4 ply.*

NEEDLES

U.S. size 2 (2.75 mm): set of 4 double-pointed (dpn). Adjust needle size if necessary to obtain the correct gauge.

NOTIONS

Removable marker (m); waste yarn for provisional CO; stitch holder (optional); thin elastic or ribbon(optional); tapestry needle.

GAUGE

13 sts and 16 rows = 2" (5 cm) in St st.

Feathered Fagoting: (4 sts)

RND 1: K2, yo, ssk.

RND 2: K2tog, yo, k2.

Rep Rnds 1 and 2 for patt.

....

Narrow Gathered Lace: (10 sts)

RND 1: K5, yo, k5.

RND 2: K3, k2tog, drop previous row's yo, yo 2 times, ssk, k3.

RND 3: K2, k2tog, drop previous row's yo's, yo 3 times, ssk, k2.

RND 4: K1, k2tog, drop previous row's yo's, yo 4 times, ssk, k1.

RND 5: K2tog, drop previous row's yo's, CO 3 sts onto right needle using the backward-loop method (see page 55), insert left needle under all 4 yo loops from front to back and (k1, yo, k1) into them, CO 3 sts onto right needle, ssk.

RND 6: K4, ssk, k5.

Rep Rnds 1–6 for patt.

....

Wide Gathered Lace: (12 sts)

RND 1: K4, k2tog, yo, ssk, k4.

RND 2: K3, k2tog, drop previous row's yo, yo 2 times, ssk, k3.

RND 3: K2, k2tog, drop previous row's yo's, yo 3 times, ssk, k2.

RND 4: K1, k2tog, drop previous row's yo's, yo 4 times, ssk, k1.

RND 5: K2tog, drop previous row's yo's, CO 4 sts onto right needle using the backward-loop method, insert left needle under all 4 yo loops from front to back and (k1, yo, k1) into them, CO 4 sts onto right needle, ssk.

RND 6: K5, ssk, k6.

Rep Rnds 1–6 for patt.

NOTES

The lace pattern of this stocking is extremely stretchy both horizontally and vertically. Size may be customized by working more or fewer repeats of the lace pattern on the foot and before and/or after the calf increases or by changing needle sizes. Stitches may be placed on waste yarn or a circular needle to try on to ensure correct fit. When worn, fabric should be slightly stretched for best effect. Stockings will look most attractive, and stay up best, when the fabric hugs the leg and foot.

....

Though these socks look intricate, the unusual lacy pattern is extremely easy to work. It's also very stretchy, so the sock is worked over a smaller number of stitches than usual, making for a surprisingly quick knit.

....

Increases to accommodate the calf are done all in one round, by increasing the width of each vertical insertion.

Stocking
Toe
Using the invisible provisional method (see Glossary), CO 24 sts onto a single dpn. Purl 1 WS row. Work short-rows (see Glossary) as foll:

SHORT-ROW 1: (RS) Knit to last st, wrap next st, turn.

SHORT-ROW 2: (WS) Purl to last st, wrap next st, turn.

SHORT-ROW 3: Knit to 1 st before wrapped st, wrap next st, turn.

SHORT-ROW 4: Purl to 1 st before wrapped st, wrap next st, turn.

Rep Short-rows 3 and 4 six more times—8 sts unwrapped at center; 8 wrapped sts at each end.

SHORT-ROW 17: (RS) Knit to first wrapped st, knit wrapped st and its wrap tog, wrap next st, turn.

SHORT-ROW 18: (WS) Purl to first wrapped st, purl wrapped st and its wrap tog, wrap next st, turn.

Rep Short-rows 17 and 18 seven more times—no wrapped sts rem.

Foot

Undo provisional CO and place live sts onto two needles to beg working in the rnd—48 sts total. Next rnd will establish beg of rnd and needle divisions.

RND 1: Sl 1, k14, place marker (pm) for beg of rnd; Needle 1—*work Rnd 1 of Narrow Gathered Lace (see Stitch Guide) over 10 sts, p1, work Rnd 1 of Feathered Fagoting (see Stitch Guide) over 4 sts, p1; rep from * for Needles 2 and 3—16 sts each needle.

RND 2: *Work Narrow Gathered Lace over 10 sts, p1, work Feathered Fagoting over 4 sts, p1; rep from * to end.

Cont in patt until 6 reps of Narrow Gathered Lace have been worked, then work Rnds 1–5 once more, or work until foot measures about 1¾" (4.5 cm) less than desired foot length, slightly stretched, ending with Rnd 5 of Narrow Gathered Lace.

Heel

Work 33 sts in patt. Next 25 sts are heel sts (this will pass the beg-of-rnd m); leave last 24 sts on needle to be worked for leg or place on holder. Work back-and-forth on 25 heel sts as foll:

SHORT-ROW 1: (RS) K3, ssk, k19, wrap next st, turn—24 heel sts rem.

SHORT-ROW 2: (WS) P22, wrap next st, turn.

Beg with Short-Row 3 of toe, cont as for toe until no wrapped sts rem.

Leg

NEXT RND: Sl 1, k14, pm for beg of rnd; Needle 1— *work Rnd 1 of Narrow Gathered Lace over 10 sts, p1, work Rnd 1 of

Feathered Fagoting over 4 sts, p1; rep from * for Needles 2 and 3—16 sts each needle.

RND 2: *Work Narrow Gathered Lace over 10 sts, p1, work Feathered Fagoting over 4 sts, p1; rep from * to end.

Cont in patt until 6 reps of Narrow Gathered Lace have been worked, then work Rnds 1–5 once more or work until leg measures half desired height, slightly stretched, ending with Rnd 5 of Narrow Gathered Lace.

Shape Calf

NEXT RND: (Rnd 6 of Narrow Gathered Lace) *K2, M1, k2, ssk, k3, M1, k2, p1, work Rnd 2 of Feathered Fagoting over 4 sts, p1; rep from * to end—6 sts inc'd; 54 sts total; 18 sts each needle.

NEXT RND: *Work Rnd 1 of Wide Gathered Lace (see Stitch Guide) over 12 sts, p1, work Rnd 1 of Feathered Fagoting over 4 sts, p1; rep from * to end.

RND 2: *Work Wide Gathered Lace over 12 sts, p1, work Feathered Fagoting over 4 sts, p1; rep from * to end.

Cont in patt until 9 reps of Wide Gathered Lace have been worked, or until leg, slightly stretched, falls just below the knee, ending with Rnd 6 of Wide Gathered Lace.

Lace Cuff and Edging

Purl 2 rnds.

NEXT RND: (eyelet rnd) *Yo, k2tog; rep from * to end.

Knit 1 rnd. Purl 2 rnds.

PICOT BO

Using the knitted method (see page 55), *CO 2 sts onto left needle, BO 4 sts loosely; rep from * to end—no sts rem.

Finishing

Weave in loose ends. If desired, tack a row of thin elastic to interior of cuff, taking care not to let sts show on RS, or thread a narrow ribbon through eyelet rnd to use as a garter.

GLOSSARY

Abbreviations

beg(s)	begin(s); beginning
BO	bind off
CC	contrasting color
cm	centimeter(s)
cn	cable needle
CO	cast on
cont	continue(s); continuing
dec(s)	decrease(s); decreasing
dpn	double-pointed needles
foll	follow(s); following
g	gram(s)
inc(s)	increase(s); increasing
k	knit
k1f&b	knit into the front and back of same stitch
k1tbl	knit 1 through the back loop
kwise	knitwise, as if to knit
m	marker(s)
MC	main color
mm	millimeter(s)
M1	make one (increase)
p	purl
p1f&b	purl into front and back of same stitch
patt(s)	pattern(s)
psso	pass slipped stitch over
pwise	purlwise, as if to purl

rem	remain(s); remaining
rep	repeat(s); repeating
rev St st	reverse stockinette stitch
rnd(s)	round(s)
RS	right side
sl	slip
sl st	slip st (slip 1 stitch purlwise unless otherwise indicated)
ssk	slip 2 stitches knitwise, one at a time, from the left needle to right needle, insert left needle tip through both front loops and knit together from this position (1 stitch decrease)
st(s)	stitch(es)
St st	stockinette stitch
tbl	through back loop
tog	together
WS	wrong side
wyb	with yarn in back
wyf	with yarn in front
yd	yard(s)
yo	yarnover
*	repeat starting point
* *	repeat all instructions between asterisks
( )	alternate measurements and/or instructions
[ ]	work instructions as a group a specified number of times

Bind-Offs

Note: Directions for standard bind-off, modified standard bind-off, suspended bind-off, Elizabeth Zimmermann's sewn bind-off, and lace bind-off are located on pages 56–57.

I-Cord Bind-Off

With right side facing and using the knitted method, cast on three stitches (for cord) onto the end of the needle holding the stitches to be bound off (Figure 1), *k2, k2tog through back loops (the last cord stitch with the first stitch to be bound off; Figure 2), slip these three stitches back to the left needle (Figure 3), and pull the yarn firmly from the back. Repeat from * until three stitches remain on left needle and no stitches remain on right needle. Bind off remaining stitches using the standard method.

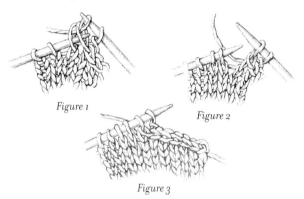

Figure 1

Figure 2

Figure 3

K2tog Bind-Off

With yarn doubled, sl 1, k1, *knit last two sts tog by inserting the left needle into the front of both sts, from left to right, and knit them tog, k1; rep from * until one st rem. Break yarn and fasten off last st.

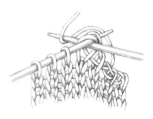

Three-Needle Bind-Off

Place the stitches to be joined onto two separate needles and hold the needles parallel so that the right sides of knitting face together. Insert a third needle into the first stitch on each of two needles (Figure 1) and knit them together as one stitch (Figure 2), *knit the next stitch on each needle the same way, then use the left needle tip to lift the first stitch over the second and off the needle (Figure 3). Repeat from * until no stitches remain on first two needles. Cut yarn and pull tail through last stitch to secure.

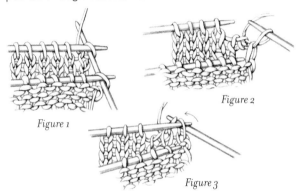

Figure 1

Figure 2

Figure 3

Blocking

Steam Blocking

Pin the pieces to be blocked to a blocking surface. Hold an iron set on the steam setting ½" (1.5 cm) above the knitted surface and direct the steam over the entire surface (except ribbing). You can get similar results by lapping wet cheesecloth on top of the knitted surface and touching it lightly with a dry iron. Lift and set down the iron gently; do not use a pushing motion. Cut blocking if you like.

Wet-Towel Blocking

Run a large bath or beach towel (or two towels for larger projects) through the rinse/spin cycle of a washing machine. Roll the knitted pieces in the wet towel(s), place the roll in a plastic bag, and leave overnight so that the knitted pieces become uniformly damp. Pin the damp pieces to a blocking surface and let air-dry thoroughly.

Cast-Ons

Note: Directions for backward-loop cast-on, knitted cast-on, and cable cast-on are located on page 55.

Crochet Chain Provisional Cast-On

With waste yarn and crochet hook, make a loose crochet chain (see page 149) about four stitches more than you need to cast on. With knitting needle, working yarn, and beginning two stitches from end of chain, pick up and knit one stitch through the back loop of each crochet chain (Figure 1) for desired number of stitches. When you're ready to work in the opposite direction, pull out the crochet chain to expose live stitches (Figure 2).

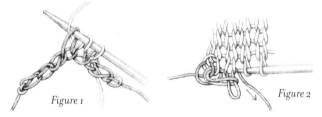

Figure 1   Figure 2

Invisible Provisional Cast-On

Make a loose slipknot of working yarn and place it on the right needle. Hold a length of contrasting waste yarn next to the slipknot and around your left thumb; hold working yarn over your left index finger. *Bring the right needle forward, then under waste yarn, over working yarn, grab a loop of working yarn and bring it forward under working yarn (Figure 1), then bring needle back behind the working yarn and grab a second loop (Figure 2). Repeat from * for the desired number of stitches. When you're ready to work in the opposite direction, place the exposed loops on a knitting needle as you pull out the waste yarn.

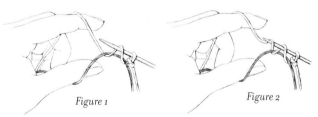

Figure 1   Figure 2

Long-Tail (Continental) Cast-On

Leaving a long tail (about ½" [1.3 cm] for each stitch to be cast on), make a slipknot and place on right needle. Place thumb and index finger of your left hand between the yarn ends so that working yarn is around your index finger and tail end is around your thumb and secure the yarn ends with your other fingers. Hold your palm upward, making a V of yarn (Figure 1). *Bring needle up through loop on thumb (Figure 2), catch first strand around index finger, and go back down through loop on thumb (Figure 3). Drop loop off thumb and, placing thumb back in V configuration, tighten resulting stitch on needle (Figure 4). Repeat from * for the desired number of stitches.

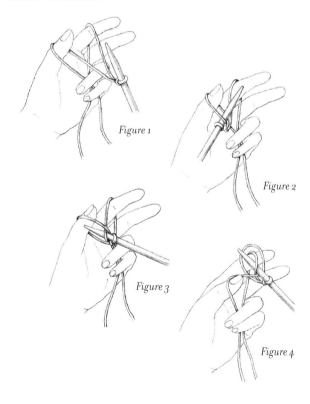

Figure 1

Figure 2

Figure 3

Figure 4

Crochet

Crochet Chain (ch)

Make a slipknot and place it on crochet hook if there isn't a loop already on the hook. *Yarn over hook and draw through loop on hook. Repeat from * for the desired number of stitches. To fasten off, cut yarn and draw end through last loop formed.

Single Crochet (sc)

*Insert hook into the second chain from the hook (or the next stitch), yarn over hook and draw through a loop, yarn over hook (Figure 1), and draw it through both loops on hook (Figure 2). Repeat from * for the desired number of stitches.

Figure 1

Figure 2

Slip-Stitch Crochet (sl st)

*Insert hook into stitch, yarn over hook and draw a loop through both the stitch and the loop already on hook. Repeat from * for the desired number of stitches.

Decreases

Knit 2 Together (k2tog)

Knit two stitches together as if they were a single stitch.

Slip 1, Knit 2 Together, Pass Slipped Stitch Over (sl 1, k2tog, psso)

Slip one stitch knitwise, knit the next two stitches together (Figure 1), then use the point of th left needle to pass the slipped stitch over the k2tog stitch and off the right needle (Figure 2).

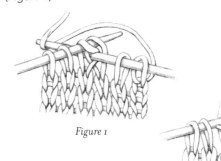

Figure 1

Figure 2

Slip, Slip, Knit (ssk)

Slip two stitches individually knitwise (Figure 1), insert left needle tip into the front of these two slipped stitches, and use the right needle to knit them together through their back loops (Figure 2).

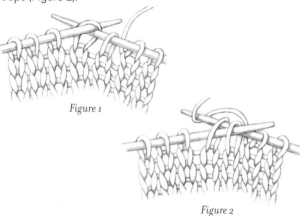

Figure 1

Figure 2

Slip, Slip, Slip, Knit (sssk)

Slip three stitches individually knitwise (Figure 1), insert left needle tip into the front of these three slipped stitches, and use the right needle to knit them together through their back loops (Figure 2).

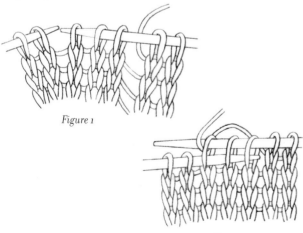

Figure 1

Figure 2

Slip, Slip, Purl (ssp)

Holding yarn in front, slip two stitches individually knitwise (Figure 1), then slip these two stitches back onto left needle (they will be turned on the needle) and purl them together through their back loops (Figure 2).

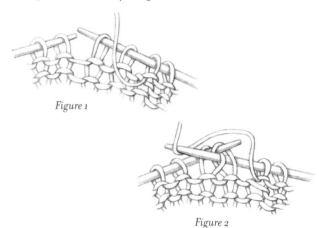

Figure 1

Figure 2

Grafting
Kitchener Stitch

Arrange stitches on two needles so that there is the same number of stitches on each needle. Hold the needles parallel to each other with wrong sides of the knitting together. Allowing about ½" (1.3 cm) per stitch to be grafted, thread matching yarn on a tapestry needle. Work from right to left as follows:

Step 1. Bring tapestry needle through the first stitch on the front needle as if to purl and leave the stitch on the needle (Figure 1).

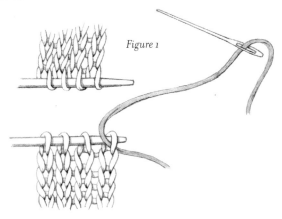

Figure 1

Step 2. Bring tapestry needle through the first stitch on the back needle as if to knit and leave that stitch on the needle (Figure 2).

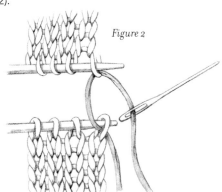

Figure 2

Step 3. Bring tapestry needle through the first front stitch as if to knit and slip this stitch off the needle, then bring tapestry needle through the next front stitch as if to purl and leave this stitch on the needle (Figure 3).

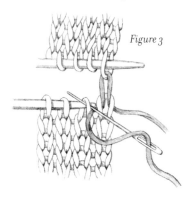

Figure 3

Step 4. Bring tapestry needle through the first back stitch as if to purl and slip this stitch off the needle, then bring tapestry needle through the next back stitch as if to knit and leave this stitch on the needle (Figure 4).

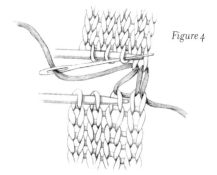

Figure 4

Repeat Steps 3 and 4 until one stitch remains on each needle, adjusting the tension to match the rest of the knitting as you go. To finish, bring tapestry needle through the front stitch as if to knit and slip this stitch off the needle, then bring tapestry needle through the back stitch as if to purl and slip this stitch off the needle.

I-Cord (also called Knit-Cord)

Using two double-pointed needles, cast on the desired number of stitches (usually three to four). *Without turning the needle, slide stitches to other end of needle, pull the yarn around the back, and knit the stitches as usual. Repeat from * for desired length.

Increases

Bar Increase (k1f&b)

Knit into a stitch but leave it on the left needle (Figure 1), then knit through the back loop of the same stitch (Figure 2) and slip the original stitch off the needle (Figure 3).

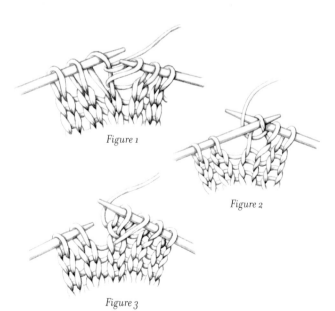

Figure 1

Figure 2

Figure 3

Lifted Increase—Left Slant

Insert left needle tip into the back of the stitch below the stitch just knitted (Figure 1), then knit this stitch (Figure 2).

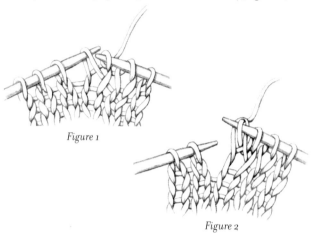

Figure 1

Figure 2

Lifted Increase—Right Slant

Note: If no slant direction is specified, use the right slant.

Knit into the back of the stitch (in the "purl bump") in the row directly below the stitch on the needle (Figure 1), then knit the stitch on the needle (Figure 2), and slip the original stitch off the needle.

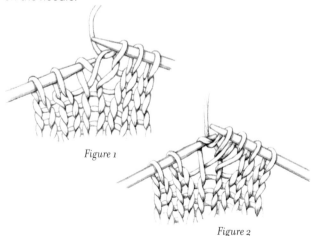

Figure 1

Figure 2

Raised Make One—Left Slant (M1L)

Note: Use the left slant if no direction of slant is specified.

With left needle tip, lift the strand between the last knitted stitch and the first stitch on the left needle from front to back (Figure 1), then knit the lifted loop through the back (Figure 2).

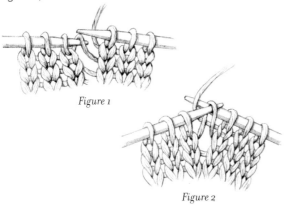

Figure 1

Figure 2

Raised Make One—Right Slant (M1R)

With left needle tip, lift the strand between the needles from back to front (Figure 1). Knit the lifted loop through the front (Figure 2).

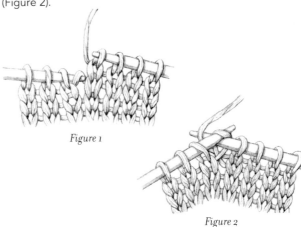

Figure 1

Figure 2

Raised Make One Purlwise (M1 pwise)

With left needle tip, lift the strand between the needles from back to front (Figure 1), then purl the lifted loop through the front (Figure 2).

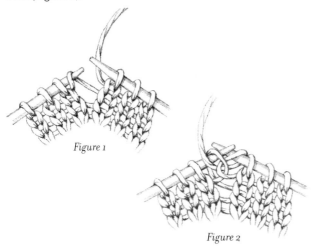

Figure 1

Figure 2

P1f&b

Purl into a stitch but leave it on the left needle (Figure 1), then purl through the back loop of the same stitch (Figure 2) and slip the original stitch off the needle.

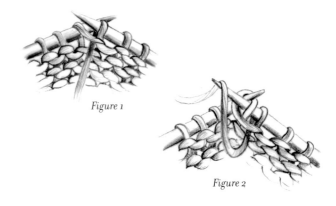

Figure 1

Figure 2

Pick Up and Knit
Pick Up and Knit

With right side facing and working from right to left, insert the tip of the needle into the center of the stitch below the bind-off or cast-on edge (Figure 1), wrap yarn around needle, and pull through a loop (Figure 2). Pick up one stitch for every existing stitch.

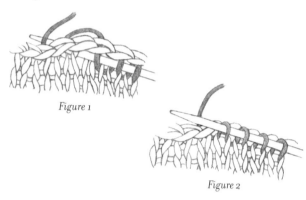

Figure 1

Figure 2

Pick Up and Knit Along Shaped Edge

With right side facing and working from right to left, insert tip of needle between last and second-to-last stitches, wrap yarn around needle, and pull through a loop. Pick up and knit about three stitches for every four rows, adjusting as necessary so that picked-up edge lays flat.

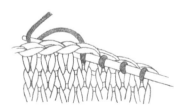

Pick Up and Purl

With wrong side of work facing and working from right to left, *insert needle tip under stitch from the far side to the near side, wrap yarn around needle (Figure 1), and pull a loop through (Figure 2). Repeat from * for desired number of stitches.

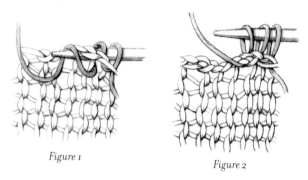

Figure 1

Figure 2

Short-Rows
Short-Rows Knit Side

Work to turning point, slip next stitch purlwise (Figure 1), bring the yarn to the front, then slip the same stitch back to the left needle (Figure 2), turn the work around and bring the yarn in position for the next stitch—one stitch has been wrapped and the yarn is correctly positioned to work the next stitch. When you come to a wrapped stitch on a subsequent row, hide the wrap by working it together with the wrapped stitch as follows: Insert right needle tip under the wrap (from the front if

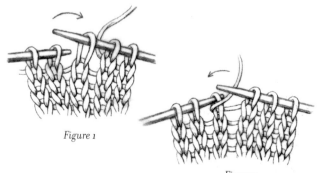

Figure 1

Figure 2

wrapped stitch is a knit stitch; from the back if wrapped stitch is a purl stitch; Figure 3), then into the stitch on the needle, and work the stitch and its wrap together as a single stitch.

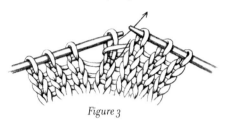

Figure 3

Short-Rows Purl Side

Work to the turning point, slip the next stitch purlwise to the right needle, bring the yarn to the back of the work (Figure 1), return the slipped stitch to the left needle, bring the yarn to the front between the needles (Figure 2), and turn the work so that the knit side is facing—one stitch has been wrapped and the yarn is correctly positioned to knit the next stitch. To hide the wrap on a subsequent purl row, work to the wrapped stitch, use the tip of the right needle to pick up the wrap from the back, place it on the left needle (Figure 3), then purl it together with the wrapped stitch.

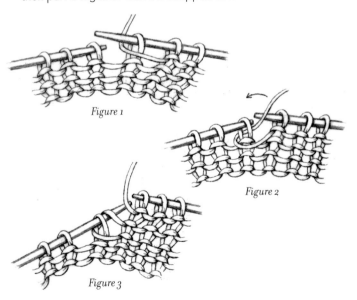

Figure 1

Figure 2

Figure 3

Twisted Cord

Cut several lengths of yarn about five times the desired finished cord length. Fold the strands in half to form two equal groups. Anchor the strands at the fold by looping them over a doorknob. Holding one group in each hand, twist each group tightly in a clockwise direction until they begin to kink. Put both groups in one hand, then release them, allowing them to twist around each other counterclockwise. Smooth out the twists so that they are uniform along the length of the cord. Knot the ends.

CONTRIBUTORS

VÉRONIK AVERY is the author of *Knitting 24/7* and *Knitting Classic Style*. Her work has appeared in books including *Knitting Green, Color Style*, and *Wrap Style*, and the magazines *Twist Collective* and *Vogue Knitting*. She is the owner of St-Denis Yarns, a yarn line distributed by Classic Elite Yarns. Avery lives in Montreal.

KAREN BAUMER lives in San Francisco, California, where she works as a linguist specializing in information retrieval, litigation support, and educational test development for verbal skills and foreign language exams.

ANN BUDD is the best-selling author of *The Knitter's Handy Book of Patterns* and *The Knitter's Handy Book of Sweater Patterns*. She is also the author of *Sock Knitting Master Class, Getting Started Knitting Socks, Interweave Presents Knitted Gifts, Knitting Green*, and *Simple Style*. Ann is a book editor and former senior editor of *Interweave Knits*. She lives in Boulder, Colorado.

NANCY BUSH is the author of *Folk Socks, Folk Knitting in Estonia, Knitting on the Road, Knitting Vintage Socks*, and *Knitted Lace of Estonia*. Her designs and articles have appeared in *Interweave Knits, Spin•Off, PieceWork, Vogue Knitting*, and *Threads*. She owns The Wooly West, a mail-order and online yarn business in Salt Lake City, Utah.

CONNIE CHANG CHINCHIO holds a PhD in physics, works 9–5 in finance, and also designs popular knitwear. Her patterns have appeared in *Interweave Knits* and *Knitscene*; she has also designed for Classic Elite, Reynolds, *Twist Collective, Knit.1*, and *Knitter's*. She lives in Jersey City, New Jersey, where she is working on her first book, *Textured Stitches*.

EVELYN A. CLARK is addicted to lace knitting and delights in sharing her addiction with others. She is the author of *Knitting Lace Triangles*, and her designs have appeared in *Spin•Off* magazine, *Knitter's Book of Wool, Sock Knitting Master Class*, and the *Vogue Knitting on the Go* series. You can find her work at evelynclarkdesigns.com.

KAT COYLE is an artist and designer who lives in Los Angeles with her son, Felix. Her book *Boho Baby Knits* features clothes and toys for little bohemians. For more about Kat, visit katcoyle.com.

CELESTE CULPEPPER has been knitting for decades and lives in Nelson, British Columbia. Visit her website at celesteknits.ca.

DONNA DRUCHUNAS is the author of six books including *Arctic Lace, Successful Lace Knitting, Ethnic Knitting Discovery*, and *Ethnic Knitting Explorations*. She lives at the foot of the Rocky Mountains in Colorado with her husband, mother, and three cats. Visit her website at sheeptoshawl.com.

JACKIE ERICKSON-SCHWEITZER is a long-time knitting enthusiast who shares her love of knitting and experience through arts organizations, classes, and networking with other fiber artists. She is the proprietor of knitwear design company HeartStrings FiberArts.

RACHEL ERIN lives in South Bend, Indiana, with her husband and two daughters. You can always find her at rachelerin.com, doing things by hand to make every day more beautiful.

ANGELA HAHN'S designs have appeared in online and print magazines including *Twist Collective, Vogue Knitting*, and *Knit.1*, and in the books *Brave New Knits, Expectant Little Knits*, and *More Big Girl Knits*. She blogs at knititude.com.

ANNE HANSON is the designer and owner of Knitspot.com. Her designs have appeared in *Knitty* and *Twist Collective* and in the books *Brave New Knits, Sock Club,* and *Sock Knitting Master Class.*

EUNNY JANG is editor of *Interweave Knits* and co-host of *Knitting Daily TV.* In the rare times that she isn't knitting or editing, Eunny cooks, runs long distance, wakeboards, and follows the Yankees from her home in Fort Collins, Colorado.

HANA JASON eats, sleeps, and breathes knitting in the Mountain West, where the wind blows cold and layers always makes sense.

KATHLEEN POWER JOHNSON'S designs have appeared in *Wrap Style, Scarf Style,* and numerous other books as well as in the magazines *Interweave Crochet, Creative Knitting,* and *Knitter's.* She lives in Sarasota, Florida.

SUSAN PIERCE LAWRENCE lives and knits in the shadow of Utah's beautiful Wasatch Mountains. You can find more of her work at knittingasfastasican.com.

FAINA LETOUTCHAIA was born in St. Petersburg, Russia, where she started designing and knitting her own garments in middle school. Her work has appeared in *Handknit Holidays* and *All New Homespun Handknit.* She lives in East Lansing, Michigan.

ANNIE MODESITT is the author of *Knit with Courage, Live with Hope; 1,000 Fabulous Knit Hats; Romantic Hand Knits,* and several other books. Her knitting and crochet designs have appeared in *Interweave Crochet, Vogue Knitting, Knit.1,* and *Knitscene* and the books *Stitch 'n' Bitch, Scarf Style, Lace Style, Folk Style, Wrap Style, Knitknit, Handknit Holidays,* and *Crocheted Gifts.* She blogs at modeknit.com.

MANDY MOORE is senior technical editor for *Knitty* and coauthor of *Yarn Bombing: The Art of Crochet and Knit Graffiti.* Her knit and crochet designs have appeared in the books *Knitting Plus* and *Not Your Mama's Crochet* and in *Interweave Crochet* and *Knitscene* magazines.

DEBBIE NEW is the author of *Unexpected Knitting.* Her work has appeared in *Knitting Art; Socks, Socks, Socks; The Natural Knitter;* and *Reversible Knitting.* She lives in Waterloo, Ontario.

SHIRLEY PADEN is the owner and founder of Shirley Paden Custom Knits and the author of the best-selling *Knitwear Design Workshop.* She teaches master design classes and conducts seminars on lace, entrelac, cables, color knitting, and finishing techniques. She lives in New York City.

GAYLE ROEHM knits, spins, and dabbles in other fiber arts in suburban Maryland. She's a former management consultant who loves travel almost as much as she loves knitting. Her designs have appeared in *A Gathering of Lace* and other publications.

SARAH SWETT knits, spins, laughs, weaves tapestries, and drinks tea with friends in Moscow, Idaho. Her knitwear designs have appeared in *Spin•Off, All New Homespun Handknit,* and *Knitting in America.* She is the author of *Kids Weaving.*

YARN SOURCES

Alchemy Yarns of
Transformation
PO Box 1080
Sebastopol, CA 95473
(707) 823-3276
alchemyyarns.com
Silken Straw

The Alpaca Yarn Company
144 Roosevelt Ave.
Bay #1
York, PA 17401
(866) 440-PACA
thealpacayarnco.com
Suri Elegance

Blue Moon Fiber Arts
56587 Mollenhour Rd.
Scappoose, OR 97056-8203
(503) 922-3431
bluemoonfiberarts.com
Luscious Silk

Elann
United States:
PO Box 1018
Point Roberts, WA 98281
Canada:
PO Box 18125
1215C-56th St.
Delta, BC V4L 2M4
(604) 952-4096
elann.com
*Den-M-Nit Pure Indigo
Cotton; Peruvian Highland
Chunky*

Gedifra
Distributed in the U.S. by
Westminster Fibers Inc.
165 Ledge St.
Nashua, NH 03060
(800) 445-9276
westminsterfibers.com
Amara

Jacques Cartier Clothier
PO Box 22
Banff, AB
Canada T1L 1A2
(403) 762-5445
qiviuk.com
Qiviuk

Jade Sapphire
(866) 857-3897
jadesapphire.com
*Lacey Lamb
Silk/Cashmere*

JaggerSpun
PO Box 188
5 Water St.
Springvale, ME 04083
(207) 324-4455
jaggeryarn.com
Zephyr

Lorna's Laces
4229 North Honore St.
Chicago, IL 60613
(773) 935-3803
lornaslaces.net
Helen's Lace

Louet North America
3425 Hands Rd.
Prescott, ON
Canada K0E 1T0
(613) 925-4502
louet.com
*Gems Merino Fingering
Weight; Gems Merino Sport
weight*

Misti Alpaca
PO Box 2532
Glen Ellyn, IL 60138-2532
(888) 776-YARN
mistialpaca.com
Lace

Reynolds/Great American
Yarns
JCA Crafts Inc.
35 Scales Ln.
Townsend, MA 01469-1094
(978) 597-8794
jcacrafts.com
Soft Sea Wool

Rowan Yarns
Distributed by Westminster
Fibers Inc.
165 Ledge St.
Nashua, NH 03060
(800) 445-9276
westminsterfibers.com
*Denim; Lima; Purelife Organic
Cotton 4 ply; Pure Wool 4
ply; RYC Cashcotton 4 ply
(discontinued); RYC Cashsoft
4 ply; RYC Siena*

Schoeller Esslinger
(now Schoeller + Stahl)
Distributed in the U.S. by Skacel
Collection Inc.
PO Box 88110
Seattle, WA 98138-2110
(800) 255-1278
skacelknitting.com
*Fortissima Cotton (discontinued);
Fortissima Socka Cotton*

Tilli Tomas
72 Woodland Rd.
Jamaica Plain, MA 02130
(617) 524-3330
tillitomas.com
Fil de la Mer

Tahki Stacy Charles
70-30 80th St. Bldg. 36
Ridgewood, NY 11385
(800) 338-YARN
tahkistacycharles.com
Tahki New Tweed

The Wooly West
PO Box 58306
Salt Lake City, UT 84158
(888) 487-9665
woolywest.com
Horizons

Twisted Sisters
Distributed by Yarnmarket.com
(888) 996-9276
twistedsistersknitting.com
Impressionist Zazu

INDEX

Explore the time-honored tradition of knitted lace

WITH THESE CLASSIC RESOURCES FROM INTERWEAVE

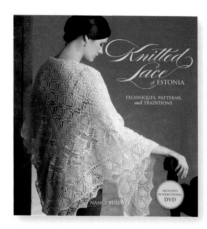

Knitted Lace of Estonia with DVD

Nancy Bush

ISBN 978-1-59668-315-0
$26.95

Lace Style

Traditional to Innovative,
21 Inspired Designs to Knit

Ann Budd and Pam Allen

ISBN 978-159668-028-9
$24.95

Wrapped in Lace

Knitted Heirloom Designs
from Around the World

Margaret Stove

ISBN 978-1-59668-227-6
$26.95

INTERWEAVE KNITS

From cover to cover, *Interweave Knits* magazine presents great projects for the beginner to the advanced knitter. Every issue is packed full of captivating smart designs, step-by-step instructions, easy-to-understand illustrations, plus well-written, lively articles sure to inspire. **Interweaveknits.com**

Join Knittingdaily.com, an online community that shares your passion for knitting. You'll get a free e-newsletter, free patterns, projects store, a daily blog, event updates, galleries, tips and techniques, and more. Sign up for *Knitting Daily* at **Knittingdaily.com**

shop.knittingdaily.com